REDS

Photography by

John M. Dibbs

Acknowledgements

A display by the 'Red Arrows' is only made possible by teamwork and the vital contribution of numerous individuals — the same is true of this volume.

I would like to thank the Team and the various members whose skill and commitment have not only made this book possible,
but have made it an honour and enjoyable privilege to create, over the past four seasons.

I am indebted to **Adrian Gjertsen** for his introduction to the Team, via **Eric Ward** and **Ray Thilthorpe** at the Red Arrows Trust,
who assisted greatly throughout, as well as **Personnel and Training Command's PR, Sqn Ldr Tony Cunnane**
and **Air Commodore Gordon McRobbie**, his Office and staff.

Special thanks to **John Rands** who not only inspired me but has created a wonderful text,
and gave me my first opportunity to fly under his tenure of leadership.

Thanks also to the cameraship pilots whose patience and skill allowed me to create the images I had envisaged.
It has been a great privilege to loop in the skies sitting behind the likes of:-

**Sqn Ldr Mike Williams, Flt Lt Dave Stobie, Wg Cdr Dick Johnson, Sqn Ldr Kelvin Truss, Flt Lt Richie Matthews, Flt Lt Sean Perrett,
Flt Lt Andy Cubin, Sqn Ldr Andy Offer, Flt Lt Ian Smith, Flt Lt Dick Patounis, Sqn Ldr Andy Lewis and Spike Jepson.**
A special mention to **Dan** 'Blue One' **Griffith**.

Talking of blue, the engineering 'blues', from the public's perspective, are a much overlooked part of the Team. Thanks to all the engineers who support
the Team unfailingly every season, and whose input is not visible in this 'from the cockpit' account, aside from the fact that there are always at least nine
jets flying! My personal appreciation to **Sqn Ldr Jon Russell, Spike Robertson** and **Jeff Sewell.** For the majority of this book the Team was led by
Sqn Ldr Simon Meade, and to him I owe a great debt for accommodating the numerous requests and 'triv' that a project like this generates.
I also owe **Dave Stobie, Gary Waterfall, Andy Offer** and **Richie Matthews** a pint!

For their support, I am grateful to **Ray Hanna, Wg Cdr Terry Yarrow, Air Commodore Simon Bostock** and **Sqn Ldr Tony Cunnane.**
David Gilmour, Norman Lees and **Brendan Walsh** at Intrepid Aviation, **Tim Manna** at Kennet Aviation.
Pam Dibbs, Rachel Wisby at The Plane Picture Company, **Darren Baker** and **Allan Burney.**

Photographic support was kindly provided by **Graham Armitage** at **Sigma**, **Peter Bowerman** at CCS Holdalls and **John Dickens** at **Pentax** (UK)

This book is dedicated to **May** and **Liam Harris** who have been there from the beginning, and whose example has,
and will, guide both Pam and myself through it all.

John M. Dibbs

———

Copyright © 1999 John Dibbs

First published in the UK in 1999 by Airlife Publishing Ltd

British Library Cataloguing-in-Publication Data

A catalogue record for this book is available from the British Library

ISBN 1 84037 121 8

Photographs ©1999 John M. Dibbs

Text ©1999 John Rands

Design and Concept by John M. Dibbs   Reprographics - 'Toad' at The Plane Picture Group

Page Layout by Karen Baker

Printed in Spain

Airlife Publishing Ltd
101 Longden Road, Shrewsbury, SY3 9EB, England
E-mail: airlife@airlifebooks.com

REDS

Airlife
England

REDS

Photography
John M. Dibbs

Text
John Rands

CONTENTS

Foreword

It is now over 30 years since the 'Red Arrows' were formed as the premier aerobatic team of the Royal Air Force.

Times change and perhaps the perceived rather cavalier style of those early years (personified by the first team leader, Lee Jones, writing in the Royal Air Force Safety Review — 'belt down the runway, hanging from my bootcaps, snatch the rose from behind the lady's ear, sometimes I get the ear too'), have also changed. None-the-less, the disciplined skills, the airmanship and showmanship required of any successful team, then as now, remain paramount.

The 'Arrows' were formed in 1965 following the earlier demise of established Fighter Command teams of Hunters and then Lightnings — mainly for reasons of cost. The tradition was continued by the Central Flying School for a couple of years fielding a Jet Provost team — the 'Red Pelicans' — which however well flown could never compete with the raw power, 'guts and glory', big metal of a nine-ship Lightning team.

The Gnat was therefore a compromise — in all respects — as was the first 'Red Arrows' team. Born via the formation of the 'Yellow Jacks'; the 'Arrows' were formed in early 1965 and set-up home at Kemble in Gloucestershire, a place of many happy memories. The work was always disciplined, light-hearted, absorbing and sometimes very concentrated; there was 'no time for a rest', lots of 'smoke on the ground', some 'wiring' and plenty of criticism from all

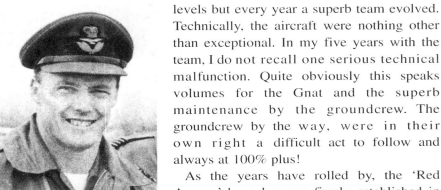

levels but every year a superb team evolved. Technically, the aircraft were nothing other than exceptional. In my five years with the team, I do not recall one serious technical malfunction. Quite obviously this speaks volumes for the Gnat and the superb maintenance by the groundcrew. The groundcrew by the way, were in their own right a difficult act to follow and always at 100% plus!

As the years have rolled by, the 'Red Arrows' have become firmly established in the eye of the public and across the world, in particular with their various and extended tours of the USA, Asia and Australia. The Hawk replaced the Gnat in 1980 and remains with the team for the foreseeable future.

From Gnats to Hawks, the 'Red Arrows' have evolved over the years with a display tailored to their aircraft. In true RAF style, they have entertained stage left, right and mostly crowd centre, to the delight of millions.

Through the stunning images of John Dibbs and the first hand account of John Rands you have in your hands a truly exceptional volume, giving an insight into the Team and it's workings, the excitement and sheer hard work that go into making the 'Red Arrows' such an elite outfit.

Long may their success continue.

Ray Hanna

Opposite:
Three Gnats and a Hawk — 'Reds Arrows' lineage beautifully depicted by the Folland Gnat in RAF Training Command colours, Yellowjacks livery, and finally in the famous scarlet overcoat of the RAF Aerobatic Team, formating on a Hawk

Photographer's Note

Everyone is familiar with the nine brightly coloured aircraft cutting through the deep blue sky — the trailing smoke painting the heavens in elegant, definite strokes. The jets whirl around the overhead in various formations — effortlessly precise — as if stuck on a perfectly clear sheet of glass. Quite simply, the sight and sound of the 'Red Arrows' in action is unforgettable.

Therefore, it was with much relish that I flew to Akrotiri in Cyprus four years ago, to undertake an assignment for the magazine *Aircraft Illustrated*.

I was seduced by the team's laid back air of confidence. I'd watched many a 'Reds' display — growing up with the legend, and looking forward to swirling around the sky in lazy circles, occasionally exposing the odd frame, just letting the world twirl around my cockpit. Some 15 minutes of practise flying later, a rather pale, sweat-soaked photo-journalist emerged from the Hawk. I'd lost count of the rivets I'd noticed on the surrounding aircraft and exhausted myself bracing against the 'G' whilst trying to compose my camera — and my head.

The story inside the formation, I'd found out, is rather different to the illusion created for the ground. The familiar nine-ship formation is more generally eight aircraft chasing one — Red Leader. He is flying a smooth and accurate pattern that allows the others to follow. He is continually adjusting his path to make sure the team appears over the crowd at the same point on every pass, snappily calling the manoeuvres and changes in direction over the R/T — giving a 'heads up' to the boys down the back. Minuscule adjustments in position by the eight and turbulence at low-level make the jets appear to thrash around when in such close proximity — so much for the sheet of glass. Streamers quite often slip from the Hawk's wingtip as the 'G' mounts rounding the bends and the rudder bar shakes in the shallower formations, caused as the tip of the fin is enveloped in jet efflux from the 'Arrow' in front. (Next time you see them parked at an airshow, look out for the discoloration of the white on the fin — caused by the smoke dye.) Sometimes the jets are only 18 inches depth separated and 4 ft nose to tail.

I got the feeling they trusted each other. To me this side of things needed to be conveyed. What better way than to let the Team tell the story? The Leader during my first flight was Sqn Ldr John Rands, with whom I hatched a plot to create the book you are now holding. The questions in my mind after that first trip were, 'How do you become a 'Red Arrow'? What drives you to this level of excellence and commitment?' John has allowed us to get into that mindset, by telling his personal story of his life as a 'Red Arrow' to complement the photographic package. Hopefully this is about as close as you can get to the 'Reds' without actually strapping on a Hawk. On a personal note I must say that from an early age, I was hypnotised by the 'Reds' photography of the late Arthur Gibson (an honorary 'Red Arrow') who I was fortunate enough to know and work with for a short while. His work continues to be an inspiration.

In the late 20th Century, formation aerobatics is one of the few areas of military aviation that has a global audience. A whole spectrum of brightly coloured teams operate — but at the end of the day there is only one colour . . . and that colour is **Red**.

John M. Dibbs, March 1999

● *The images in this book were created using Pentax and Canon cameras (the ergonomics proving useful at 4G), fitted with a range of Pentax, Sigma and Canon Lenses. 14mm, 18-35mm and 28-70mm were my favoured optics during the aerial work (now you can appreciate how close the 'Reds' get!). 80-200mm, 300-400mm lenses provided the focal length required on the ground. Fuji Velvia stock delivered the colour and CCS Holdalls secured the equipment. My technique involved Auto exposure, generally with no filtration — a canopy gets in the way enough. All the Velvia was processed by PDQ Laboratories, Bushey.*

Preface

When John Dibbs suggested that I write the words to accompany the beautiful aerial images that he has captured of the 'Red Arrows', I tentatively agreed and set about wondering how I could match in words what he has so wonderfully captured through the camera lens. In viewing his images I was immediately transported back into the cockpit that had been my second home for many years, and from where I had been privileged to fly alongside some of the UK's finest military pilots.

Although I left the world of fast-jet flying only a short time ago, I am humbled by just how much I have forgotten. I never thought that the thrill and excitement of nearly 20 years of military aviation could ever be anything other than the crystal sharp images of people, places, and, of course, aeroplanes. But I soon found that I had to rely more on the entries in my old flying logbooks and brief glimpses at photo albums to recall significant events — which saddens me. Maybe by writing something down now before I forget completely, my children may one day read where their dad was during the long absences from home that were, and still are, the norm for today's RAF pilots.

Although this story relates to my own personal experiences within the RAF, it is by no means unique. Service pilots, past and present, will recognise the highs and lows that are all part of fast-jet flying. It is their story as well as mine.

So where to begin? For me it all started in my hometown of Scunthorpe . . . .

John Rands

Born to Fly

I say, I say, I say. Have you heard the one about Scunthorpe, the smog and the steel worker's daughter? No, neither have I, but then if you were brought up in Scunthorpe in the 1960s, you became accustomed to the constant stream of music-hall jokes directed at this gritty Lincolnshire steel town. Despite the jibes, it was a happy place to grow up . . . and aviation was never far away.

My father had served in the Fleet Air Arm in the late forties and early fifties and possessed two old photograph albums of wonderful black and white images of Royal Navy aircraft. I spent so many hours poring over these images, that even now I can probably still identify every different type and squadron — and perhaps even the airfield over which it flew.

One summer during my early years, I went with my family to one of the steelwork's galas held on the northern end of town. Here, apart from the funfair and sporting events, the RAF appeared with some of their latest and noisiest machines. I watched the earth-shaking Vulcan pirouette and dance just above my head, whilst conversation for hundreds of yards around was made impossible by the noise of its engines. Later, just as my ears were responding to sound, a Lightning appeared and again my rib cage resonated in concert with the deafening onslaught. Unlike the lumbering Vulcan, this silver dart flashed across the sky like a swallow until, tiring of being watched by mere mortals, it pointed towards the heavens and left us all staring into space as it rapidly became a small black dot in the dark blue overcast. No matter how hard I squinted, the Lightning had disappeared completely from view — but the heavens still reverberated with its presence.

Whilst idly leaning back in my school chair one afternoon, as the summer warmth sapped the noise from the normally chaotic classroom, there was an almighty bang that shook the windows and startled every dreamy child into animated life. Teachers rushed from room to room to see if we were intact and check that our windows were still in place. Although we didn't know it at the time, we had just been subjected to a sonic boom from some high flying fighter. Years later when wrestling to ensure that my Lightning remained the right side of the sound-barrier during combat sorties, I knew what those unfortunate souls on the ground would be subjected to if I let the old girl get away from me.

Such was my fascination for all things in aviation, that I soon became involved with the local Air Training Corps Squadron, even though I was far too young to be officially admitted. At the time I was only 12, and was unceremoniously informed that I needed to be a good two years older before I could enrol and be issued with the wonderfully ill-shaped blue serge uniform. Even now I can still smell the overpowering odour of sweat and mothballs that came free with every issue from the uniform store; the smell of an entire squadron caught out in a rain shower was enough to cause offence to even the hardiest soul. Undeterred, I rarely missed any of the two parade nights each week. Eventually the Commanding Officer was worn down by my persistence and allowed me amongst the uniformed ranks, many months before I should have officially joined.

I was completely hooked. They even allowed young fellows like me to fly in real aeroplanes and gliders, fire rifles that were far too big for me, and go away for a week at a time to real RAF Stations — where, if we were really lucky, we could sweep hangar floors and polish real aeroplanes. What more could a young aviation crazy youth have wished for!

By now I knew that there was only one thing I wanted to do in adult life, and spent the next five years dreaming and scheming of how I was going to be accepted into the RAF. I made the mistake of letting the careers adviser at school into my plans. 'No' she chided, 'the chances of someone from a comprehensive school being accepted as an officer into the RAF were quite remote; start thinking about a trade on the steelworks young man'. If only I could meet her now.

At the age of 16, I was selected by the Air Cadets to undertake glider pilot training at the local airfield. This was the stuff of dreams. Of course I was more than a little nervous, for

Opposite: Intrepid Aviation's beautifully preserved
Folland Gnat in Yellowjack colours

instead of sitting alongside the instructor as I had done many times on passenger rides in the past, I was now expected to soak up professional flying instruction . . . . and then fly the machine on my own.

And what machines they were. Not for us the highly polished sleek machines that adorn the English summer skies today; these were from an earlier era. The Kirby Cadet Mk 3 and the Slingsby Sedbergh were the backbone of the Air Cadet gliding organisation and were revered for their viceless handling characteristics that built confidence in young petrified chaps like me. They wouldn't have won any prizes for elegance or performance, but they were robust simple machines that probably hoisted more first-time solos aloft than any other post-war type.

The venue for my early flying training was RAF Lindholme just to the East of Doncaster. Sadly, it is now one of the innumerable new prisons, but then it was a former WW2 bomber base that had more recently been the home of the men who were trained to fly Britain's nuclear bombers. By the mid-1970s it was surplus to requirements and only a handful of families still lived amongst its sprawling married quarters. The Air Training Corps based one of its gliding schools in the hangars that had once protected the mighty Lancaster and Halifax bombers.

These were very happy days. Every weekend I would hitch-hike the 20 or so miles to the airfield to work either as a winch driver or a general dogsbody, in the vain hope of being rewarded at the day's end with a quick trip around the circuit. In fact, by now I was so completely obsessed with flying that all other tasks were secondary, much to the dismay of my teachers. I would idly spend my maths lessons looking dreamily at the heavens and willing the painfully long school week to end and the weekend to begin.

Thankfully I didn't manage to forego all of my education; for in the summer of 1978 I attended the RAF's Officer and Aircrew Selection Centre at Biggin Hill — along with dozens of other aspiring young aviators. Weeks later, after what seemed like an absolute eternity, I received a single sheet of A5 paper in a very official looking brown envelope, informing me that I would be called forward to begin my RAF training in due course. I can still recall the look of perplexed amusement on the face of the principal at my sixth form college, probably wondering how the RAF had chosen me when there were so many more suitable candidates around.

Learning the Trade

Hitchin railway station in 1978 was no different from any other dreary British Rail establishment. It was to this small part of Bedfordshire on a dull November afternoon that I stepped off the train to begin my new life in the RAF. There was, however, one major obstacle between the transformation required from pimply faced youth to lantern-jawed defender of the faith, and this was the Officer Cadet Training Unit at RAF Henlow — now just a short bus ride away.

Collecting us from the station was a youth who I estimated was about my age, but there any similarity ended. He was dressed in Air Force Blue and had the sharpest creases in his trousers and the shiniest shoes I had ever seen. But worse was yet to come. On arrival at the Mess at Henlow, this youth removed his hat to reveal an almost baldhead. He obviously sensed our looks of incredulity and promised that, all things being equal, by lunchtime the following day we would all be sporting similar hairstyles, or in this case, lack of.

Sadly he was right, and the next morning's visit to the barber set the seal on 18 weeks of marching, running, writing, parading, and generally a whole host of activities that could not have been further removed from learning to fly. Many times during those long winter nights as I lay cradling my rifle whilst lying in the middle of some freezing forest, did I wonder if I might have joined the Army by mistake.

Somehow, against all the odds and my immature teenage years, I passed out of Henlow in the spring of 1979, with many friends who would accompany me through one of the great adventures in my life, RAF flying training. I'm not sure that the world was quite ready for the bunch of desperately keen Acting Pilot Officers who now headed north to form Number 40 Course at RAF Linton-on-Ouse.

Jet-propelled

RAF Linton-on-Ouse lies just a few miles to the West of the beautiful and historic city of York and is still, today, the home of one of the RAF's basic flying training schools. Here in the summer of 1979, 18 members of Number 40 course gathered to begin a year of intense training on the Jet Provost. The previous months of hard physical exercise had made us fitter and leaner, but still most of us were in our late teens, had peanuts for brains, more testosterone than was good for us, and knew practically bugger all about the real world.

What we did realise though, was that we were probably the luckiest guys around. Linton was a happy place with a great social scene and a lot of flying when the partying subsided. We were taught to fly the venerable Jet Provost Mk 3, an early-generation jet trainer that was powered by a small Rolls-Royce Viper engine. The Viper engine boasted a similar power output to those hand dryers you find in public loos, but it made a great screaming jet-like noise and happily absorbed the abuse of us baby pilots. After only a few hours of instruction we were deemed far too dangerous to fly with by our instructors, and we were ordered to struggle around the circuit on our own!

In those early days, we were never allowed out of sight of the airfield, but slowly (and sometimes painfully), we started to progress to slightly more complex exercises.

Our home for these early triumphs was the relief landing ground at Elvington, a disused bomber base a few miles the other side of York. It boasted one of the longest runways in the country, having been extended to accommodate some very large American wonder bomber that had never arrived. But now thankfully it was quiet and could accept three or four trainees in the visual circuit without too much drama. Indeed the airfield was spectacularly long if you lined up pointing the right way, which occasionally, when under great personal strain, some individuals failed to do. One of our chaps, who will of course remain anonymous but now works for the Army, managed to turn 10,000ft of tarmac into something much shorter, until his instructor swung the mighty JP through 180 degrees to reveal a far more reassuring picture.

The only comfort in these early days was that we were all struggling together. Our course was generally very friendly, but the statistics of military flying training soon became apparent. One by one, our course mates were whittled away, having been unable to overcome the many training milestones; be it low-level navigation, night flying, formation flying, or sometimes just the inability to cope under pressure.

By the end of the course, only five out of the original 18 progressed to fly the Hawk at RAF Valley and the next stage of fast-jet training. Some of our friends transferred to helicopters or multi-engine aircraft, some opted to try navigator training or other RAF branches, or some simply returned to civvy street.

Hawk-eyed

RAF Valley on the island of Anglesey in North Wales isn't everybody's idea of a dream posting. For those personnel having to spend a full 3-4 year tour of duty there, the bleak winters, poor road connections that were the norm 20 years ago, and the general feeling of isolation could seem overwhelming. For the lucky chaps who formed Number 51 course in the late summer of 1980, it was just another part of the great adventure, and we were programmed only to spend six months on the edge of civilisation.

It was here that we rejoined some of our buddies from officer training who had completed their basic flying training at the RAF College Cranwell. Everyone was in high spirits and from an early stage we had the makings of a first-rate course.

The flying in the British Aerospace Hawk was simply fantastic. The aeroplanes were very shiny and new, and under the expert guidance of our long suffering instructors we set about learning to fly one of the great success stories of post-war British aviation.

If we were sometimes mediocre in the air, then we certainly excelled in the bar. The gauntlet had been thrown down by our senior course, which had managed to supply for general consumption, as many barrels of beer as their course number. To beat this magnificent achievement over the 30 weeks available, Number 51 course began the chase for fame and notoriety from the very first day.

The routine was very simple; work hard and play hard. Once the flying and studying were done for the day, we would congregate for a few beers in the bar and plan the evening's activities. We regularly raided our instructors' homes when we were least expected (or welcomed if the truth were known). The drill was quite simple, load the beer barrel and pump into the boot of a car, position it as silently as possible close to the intended victim's front door, pour the first few ales, knock on the door and wait. The sight of a dishevelled instructor, sporting slippers and a five o'clock shadow, peering out towards his worst nightmare was always a pleasure.

Often overheard in the instructor's crewroom the following morning were the cries of pain and the comment that certain members of staff weren't looking their best. 'You look bloody awful old chap, what happened', to which the reply was inevitably '51 course, that's what happened'. Murmurs of sympathy usually followed from fellow instructors who had previously suffered a similar fate, and gazes of horror from those who hadn't yet received a visit, but knew they were on the list.

By the end of six months tucked away on Anglesey, we were deemed proficient for further training, and awarded our flying brevet or 'wings' as they are universally known. The ceremony itself is focused on proud parents, as families come together to celebrate one more milestone in their son's flying career. In truth, although individuals can proudly wear the most coveted badge of office, the training system is only half-complete. From Valley, the lucky few proceeded south to be trained how to operate our little fighters that, it was assumed by now, we could safely fly.

Heaven in Devon

RAF Chivenor rightly earned the sobriquet 'Heaven in Devon' amongst those fortunate to have spent any time in this most picturesque part of the Southwest. Located on the north shore of the Taw Estuary, just to the west of Barnstaple, this little airfield sits at the gateway to some of the best low-flying regions, surrounded by fairly clear airspace, and has both air-to-air and air-to-ground weapons ranges conveniently located within a few minutes flying time.

It was here that we were taught to think aggressive thoughts, and consider how best we could use our aircraft as weapons of war. Everything we did from here on had one purpose — to put weapons on targets, at the right time, and in just about any weather.

Hung beneath the Hawk's stubby little wings, were practice-bomb carriers, and anchored firmly beneath the aircraft's belly was a 30mm Aden cannon used for both air-to-air and strafing. The weapons range at Pembrey on the South Wales coast was to be our regular playground. We tried to get the little practice

bombs close to the centre of the bombing circle, and put as many bullets through the hessian screen strafe target, without scaring our instructors or the range safety staff.

Weapon safety was drilled into us from day one, the penalty for flying outside the danger area with a live gun or weapon pylon was necessarily severe. At best you would receive a huge rollicking, at worst you could be off the course. Having seen the immensely destructive power of the weapons that the big boys got to fly with, this hard regime in training was only setting us up for what was to come later.

The emphasis also changed now from being led by others in the air, to planning, briefing, and leading a pair of aircraft on simulated attack missions. Thinking for yourself was normally difficult enough, but having to think for others in the air multiplied the workload accordingly. The learning curve was steep. Keep your aircraft at the correct height and speed; look back continually over your shoulder for the aggressor aircraft that was never far away; navigate to the targets (invariably there would be at least two); monitor the fuel; deviate off track for weather and then regain the track and timing down route; find the IP (Initial Point — normally an easily identifiable feature that led into the target); ensure you get all the weapon switchery correct and the sight through the target; and regain defensive formation off target. All this before heading home for 'tea and medals'. A lot was expected of you, as it would be for the rest of the training — it never stopped.

At the end of the Tactical Weapons course we were no longer just pilots, we had crossed the bridge towards earning our true wings as fighter pilots. The "powers that be" sat in judgement on our course and decided which front-line aircraft would be unlucky enough to receive the next bunch of young hooligans. We were to go our separate ways. The Navy chaps headed off for the Sea Harrier, the RAF chaps to the ground-attack Harrier or the Phantom. But for me it was a dream come true . . . I was posted to Binbrook to begin my five-year love affair with the magnificent Lightning.

Opposite: BAe Hawk T. 1As of No. 2 TWU RAF Chivenor

Thunder and Lightning

I had never before flown a particularly big aeroplane. In fact, if the truth be known, I had never before flown a single-seater or anything with more than one engine! All of this was about to change as I joined the Lightning Training Flight at RAF Binbrook in the autumn of 1981.

Binbrook, perched precariously on the top of the Lincolnshire Wolds, was formerly the home of the RAAF during the Second World War. After witnessing the beginning of the jet age, it was now home to the RAF's final two Lightning Squadrons. Amongst the sprawling hangars were the last remaining airframes that had once equipped nine front-line units across the UK, Germany, Cyprus and Singapore. In all there were almost 70 Lightning T5s, F3s and F6s, either in use with Nos 5 and 11 Squadrons and the Lightning Training

Flight, or stored in the rear hangars.

The Lightning Training Flight occupied the centre hangar on the waterfront, neatly separating the two squadrons. As a unit it had a handful of flying and weapons instructors, and the use of about 10 aircraft. These were primarily the bulbous-nosed two-seat T5s, with about four F3s and a single F6 used as a radar target aircraft.

As a young Flying Officer at the tender age of 21, I was completely besotted by Binbrook and the fantastic social life that revolved around the Mess with two very active squadrons in residence; but most of all, I was in love with the Lightning.

The Lightning towered above me, and just exuded raw unbridled power. It was so big that it required a gymnastic struggle up a big ladder just to access the cockpit. Avoiding the

refuelling probe half way up the ascent was crucial, and after head-butting this impressive bit of plumbing a number of times, I always wore my helmet before heading out onto the flight line. Once you had reached the cockpit sill, you looked down into a wonderful 1950's world of cramped aviation history. The Martin-Baker Mk 4 seat seemed to take up most of the limited cockpit space, with barely enough room for the human element. Once in the seat I felt the cockpit walls brushing against my shoulders and every part of the instrumentation could be touched without leaning forward.

I was one of three hopefuls who formed Number 47 course in the autumn of 1981. The course was scheduled to last between three and four months, but the simulator which accounted for an important part of the early part of the course was being modernised — well, a part of it was. The boffins that looked after the valve technology that kept everything running, had concluded that the weapon side of the business was unsupportable and needed to be updated. On paper what was suggested sounded great, but getting the 1s and 0s of the emerging digital technology to talk to the valves that controlled the flight part of the simulator proved a nightmare. The three-month upgrade lasted nearly seven, and meant that Number 47 course kicked its heels and grew increasingly frustrated.

Eventually our course began in earnest. Handling the simulator emergency drills soon qualified us to be cleared solo, but only after mastering the mighty T5.

Flying the two-seat T5 was different from anything I had attempted before. Sure the controls worked the same as in any other aircraft, but this swept-wing bullet was a million miles away from the Jet Provost and the benign little Hawk. The two Rolls-Royce Avon turbojets were from a different era, where thrust was king and fuel economy wasn't part of the vocabulary.

The T5 was almost identical to the F3, except that the cockpit had been widened to accept a second Martin-Baker ejection seat — just! Getting into the cockpit second wasn't a good option, as the instructor invariably had his backside covering half of your seat as well, and the ensuing struggle to retrieve your own straps in the battle of the elbows normally left you breathless and with skinned knuckles.

Getting the Avon engines started wasn't a subtle affair. None of those wimpy little electrical carts or air start systems — this baby used explosives. Sitting above the motors was a tank of Avpin that once you pressed the start button was literally detonated (in a semi-controlled sort of way), which in turn kicked the Avons into life. It was a suitably quick way of getting going, and the distinctive *Weeee — Pwoosh* could probably be heard 10 miles away.

From hitting the starter buttons, time was now the most important factor. Even sitting at idle on the ground, the engines were drinking the limited supply of Avtur at a prodigious rate. After-start checks were completed at the gallop, and the dash for the runway was begun almost instantly. Taxying the Lightning took some getting used to as the brake lever was on

photo: Allan Burney

the control column, and steering was achieved through differential braking. On top of this, in order to keep the air turbine that powered the electrics on line, the number 2 engine sat at an artificially high ground idle, which kept accelerating the aircraft if unchecked.

Binbrook's main runway wasn't particularly long or wide and two aircraft performing a pair's take-off seemed to cover the whole width of the runway. For the take-off, the engines were wound up to 92%, a final check was made around the office for anything out of the ordinary, and then the brakes were released as the engines were pushed all the way to full power. The T5 and F3 didn't ordinarily need reheat for

Opposite:
Lightning APC, Akrotiri, Cyprus. A youthful 'Rands' stands far right
Above:
The business end of a Lightning low over the North Sea

take-off, but the rush in full cold power was impressive enough.

The nose was lifted at 150kts, aiming to unstick at around 170kts. The biggest job then was whipping the gear up so the nose wheel was tucked away by the 250kts limit.

By comparison, the Harrier is the only aeroplane I have flown that was quicker off the blocks (stunningly quick), but the Lightning didn't run out of puff later on like the Harrier, it just kept accelerating. The climb speed was 450kts, converting to Mach 0.9 later on. Of all the old lady's party tricks, her ability to climb like a homesick angel, and then descend like a brick built outhouse in free-fall, was always one of my favourites.

I guess the real challenge to flying the Lightning in the early days was getting her back on the ground. Her highly swept wing didn't produce a huge amount of lift at low speed, which meant racing at the runway at speeds that poor people could only dream of. The finals turn was flown at 190kts, reducing to 175kts on the final approach. Landing at the right speed on the first bit of available concrete was priority number one.

Having successfully impacted the first available bit of concrete was sometimes just the start of your difficulties. One of the many operational shortcomings that the Lightning suffered from was landing at nearly 200 miles per hour on bicycle tyres without brakes. (Well there were brakes, but they usually only managed to get really hot before fading.)

To minimise using the brakes, it was normal to deploy the brake parachute soon after touchdown, and only apply the brakes to bring the old girl under control below 100kts. If the chute didn't deploy properly (quite common), then either a go around was flown, or if you were short of fuel (the norm), you stayed down and hammered the brakes. A precautionary landing was declared when short of juice. It meant that whatever happened, you didn't have the fuel to go around. You landed the aeroplane, brought both motors to idle (this meant dragging the number 2 through its high idle gate, thus losing all of the alternator-driven electrics) and started braking as you pulled the chute handle. If the chute worked you were well placed, and if it didn't you were prepared. At night with both engines at idle, the cockpit was pitch black until you got rid of the chute and brought up the number 2 engine back to high idle

for the taxi in.

Having mastered (and I use the term advisedly) the basics of handling the T5s and F3s, the real work began with the weapons phase of the course. The Lightning boasted a radar, two air-to-air missiles, and two 30mm Aden cannons. The radar was very advanced for its day, but by the early eighties it was well past its sell by date, and required two extra pairs of hands with ten fingers on each to operate it. Here we learned the intricacies of finding and assessing target tracks before manoeuvring into weapon range without looking outside the cockpit.

At the end of my time with the Lightning Training Flight, I was posted to the Eastern Hangar, which was the home of No 5 (Fighter) Squadron, and would be my home for the next four and a bit years. Just over three years since stepping off the train at Henlow, I was joining my first squadron.

Short of Gas!

After I had left the Lightning, I would often hear military aviators from different backgrounds chatting over the coffee bar about running low on fuel. Sure, being short of fuel in any aeroplane can be exciting, but the dear old Lightning was short before you had got off the blocks — once airborne it just got worse.

Often, miles away from base out over the cold unforgiving North Sea, I would regularly be homeward bound on bare minimums, knowing that however hard I looked at the fuel gauges, the picture just wouldn't get any better. The trick was to stay as high as possible as long as possible and only at the last possible minute commit down the hill for Terra Firma. Arriving on Binbrook approach frequency to hear that the weather was worse than awful and there were six ahead of you in the pattern, was always sobering. To be fair, Binbrook's 'air traffickers' were probably the best in the business, and the pattern was kept very tight, often only hitting the glide path at 1,000ft, a couple of miles behind the preceding traffic. I learned very early on that this was the way of things, and on the final approach would often ignore the distracting fuel gauges altogether — I couldn't influence them from here on.

There were the odd one or two who carried home a bit of fuel for Mum, but most accepted that to get anything useful out of the training sorties, bringing any spare juice home wasn't helping.

During exercises, the North Sea on our doorstep was often chock-a-block with dozens of different fighters, and the Binbrook Wing would contribute a large percentage of these.

The 'air war' would be updated over the telebrief fed into the cockpit during alerts, so sitting on state waiting to be scrambled you could quickly get an idea of how big the raids were, and who was airborne.

Lightning scrambles will always feature in my top 10 aviation hit list. From getting the order to go, the aeroplane could be started in seconds and moving very soon afterwards. The taxi out was at an impatient gallop, and normally well before the runway; the ever-vigilant air traffic would give you clearance to launch. Without pausing to catch breath, the throttles would be on their way forward on the final bend and as soon as the aeroplane was straightening out down the runway centreline the engines would be starting to cook nicely at full cold power. A couple of seconds to let them settle and then the throttles were rocked outboard and inched forward to the best of all settings — full burner.

The Lightning's 'hot streak' reheat ignition system opened the nozzles at the rear of the jetpipe, whilst squirting fuel at regular intervals down the jetpipe until the reheat fuel ring caught and sent you merrily on your way. The beautiful long flickering tongues of flame that were the hallmark of full reheat were always a pleasure to watch, especially at night.

As soon as the gear and flap were up, the burners were cancelled, and the race out to the aerial playground began in earnest. Always working alongside another fighter, as soon as the coast passed under our bellies we would be vectored by the fighter controllers (hunched low over their out-dated radar scopes) either to a CAP (combat air patrol) position, towards the incoming raid, or straight to the tanker.

The tankers were normally Victors out of Marham, but later on we would often meet recently-converted Vulcans, or VC10s. Air-to-air refuelling became an almost everyday event, but on exercise, instead of a dedicated slot where only your own formation was sucking-in the precious fuel, anybody (and sometimes seemingly everybody), would be crowded around the poor old tanker like hungry pigletss.

My record was arriving leading a pair of thirsty F6s to find eight other Lightnings in attendance. Two were plugged in, whilst six were stacked neatly on one wingtip. The next 15 minutes was brilliantly choreographed by one of the senior hands who quickly gripped what could have been chaotic.

'Right, who's hurting', came the call.

'23 needs to tank in the next five minutes',

'41 the same',

'25 is sucking fumes, and would like priority',

And so it went on. The guys already in contact were told to take just enough to keep them airborne, and then began an intricate dance as aircraft darted in behind the refuelling hoses like humming-birds, taking a quick drink, and then darting onto the opposite wing whilst others quickly took their place.

Soon order was restored and, as quickly as they came, pairs of fighters dropped away from the feeding gaggle to hunt out the bad guys, whilst the radio reported that other thirsty fighters were inbound.

These aerial refuelling dances normally took place around

Above: John Rands behind the stick of a Lightning.
The photograph was taken using a Jaguar's recce pod
whilst returning from an IAT at RAF Fairford

33,000ft, which seemed to suit the older technology of Victor, Vulcan and Lightning. If needed to, we could manage at higher levels. On one particularly claggy afternoon, when all the lower levels were awash with dirty grey thick cirrus, we took on fuel at 39,000ft. As the tanks filled, more and more power was required, but it was no great drama. The highest recorded refuelling during my time at Binbrook was 43,000ft by one of the older hands, but apparently, one of the burners was needed towards the end of the bracket.

By comparison, the newer jets on the street seemed to have a non-existent high-level capability, and as the 'Muds' became interested in the cloistered world of air-to-air refuelling, which had been primarily the preserve of the fighter boys, things started to change.

One winter's night, we were vectored onto a Victor at just above 20,000ft. Once established on the wing we could make out a new shape in behind the port hose. One of the first Tornado GR1s had graced us with its presence, but was at the ceiling of its refuelling capability. As the Victor rolled into a turn, the darkened shape of the GR1 started to slide backwards as it ran out of puff, only to stay engaged by use of, what appeared to be, full reheat. This unsporting gesture lit up the whole sky, and prompted a number of witty and quite cruel

comments from the old fashioned turbojet boys who, if needed, could have throttled an Avon back to idle, and managed quite comfortably on one engine at that height.

Late one winter's evening, I was airborne with my flight commander practising intercepts way up to the north of Binbrook. My flight commander was in the longer-legged F6, whilst I had drawn one of the Squadron's few short-range F 3s that were kept primarily for the high-G sorties, but would fly most of the unit's missions if required. This night, I was already over a tonne of fuel below my leader owing to the F3's smaller capacity. At the end of the mission, when I should have been pointing the nose for home, we were offered a tanker that was heading south towards its Norfolk home, but still had a couple of tonnes of fuel to give away. Once we turned to intercept, I was committed. Binbrook was now out of range, but I kept open the option of diverting into Newcastle or Leeming.

As we began talking to the controller handling the south-bound tanker, it soon became apparent that this Victor had been operating way off the coast, and our vectors began turning us away from land and the only concrete in range. The tanker became my only option of keeping in the air.

I let my leader know that I couldn't hang around with lengthy

photo: Allan Burney

joins, and needed to plug in without delay. We picked up the Victor at about 25 miles on radar and began fine-tuning our 'attack' to guarantee a tight stern intercept. Half way round the turn, I assumed the lead, and using the radar for closure information, I set off in pursuit of the life-giving hoses trailing a few feet behind the Victor's wings. The tankers generally flew at about 270kts when trailing their hoses, and the plan now was to arrive astern with just a few extra knots in hand. I guess the final approach didn't take that long, but in my cockpit, with the fuel gauges showing a pitifully small amount, it seemed to drag. Eventually out of the cluster of navigation and refuelling lights, I could make out the Victor's form and, soon after that, the hoses. I hit the hose without pausing and as the lights on the pod changed to green, I nervously eyed my fuel gauges to watch for the increase. Again time stood still, but just when I thought that it wasn't my night, the needles began to swing in the right direction.

Using the extra fuel we stayed airborne for more intercepts before heading home.

In the coffee bar later that evening, my flight commander asked if I had any comments because he reckoned I must have been a tad short heading for the tanker. 'No, well within the bracket', I replied, which I guess by Lightning standards I was!

They say that you never really forget your first true love and, as my wife has often pointed out, this for me was the Lightning. After five years as an 'Air Defender', I was ready to move on to pastures new, but I still look back on my time at Binbrook with great fondness and am regularly surprised by the emotion that this venerable old lady can still generate.

I realise now that I was very lucky to have had the opportunity to serve on one of the last Lightning squadrons. The aeroplane was everything I had dreamed of, and much, much more. Nowadays, the sort of performance that we savoured is readily available in much more civilised form, but for a 1950's design and technology, she was unbelievable.

At low fuel weights, the Lightning had a thrust-to-weight ratio of 1:1, and even at heavy weight could make your eyes water. I hear that the Tornado F3 is library-quiet at very high speed and that conversation is possible without the microphones in the oxygen masks. Not so in the Lightning. Once you arrived above 600kts, the noise and buffeting let you

know that you were hammering along. The refuelling probe didn't help matters, and reduced the legal top IAS limit considerably. In fact the upper IAS limit was not that high and the wonderfully designed air speed indicator only went up to 700kts. There was, however, a small standby ASI that, although difficult to read, would gladly show speeds well in excess of the book figures — I am reliably informed!

Air-to-air combat sorties were initiated at 15,000ft, with the first cross normally taking place just above the hard deck at 5,000ft. If the fight then went vertical, the next time you passed your opponent was normally around 35,000ft, before the fight normally slowed and spiralled down toward base height — a subsonic loop of 30,000ft!

Often in Cyprus, having finished off firing the gun against the hessian target towed by the Canberras, and not wanting to return to base immediately, I would either head off to say hello to the poor old Soviets anchored in their warships just south of the Island, or accelerate to just below the speed of sound before heading for the heavens.

With clearance from the local radar station that the airspace above was clear, the throttles were eased forward. At about Mach 0.98, the nose would be pulled into the vertical whilst the burners were engaged. The altimeter would wind like a propeller, and the rate of climb indicator would be hammered hard against the top stop. Eventually as the speed bled away and the controls loosened their grip on the rapidly thinning air, I would ease the old lady on to her back at usually well above 40,000ft. The climb had taken literally seconds. Now with a perfect view of the island below to the north and fuel again starting to run low, it was time for home.

Not only could the Lightning climb spectacularly, it could fall out of the sky like no other aeroplane I have ever flown.

One party trick was to stay at about 25,000ft until the airfield was just about to disappear under the nose. Then, by closing the throttles, extending the airbrakes whilst rolling inverted and pulling into an almost vertical dive, the height would drop off like a military pay rise, and again, seconds later, you would be heading through initials at 500ft, and 360kts as if nothing had happened. This descent into the field was known in the trade as a Tirpitz, after, one assumes, the fate of the German warship of the same name. What could be better than this. . . ?

Dreaming in Colours

The heady days at Binbrook remain etched in my mind like a treasured black and white photograph, but the era of Kodachrome was beckoning just around the corner — or, more correctly, just across the Lincolnshire Wolds. Increasingly my gaze was being drawn westwards where distant multi-colour smoke trails betrayed the presence of RAF Scampton, then home to the RAF Aerobatic Team, the 'Red Arrows'. I was more than a little bit curious.

Every year a signal would be sent around the whole of the RAF asking for volunteers with certain fast-jet experience to apply to join the following year's 'Red Arrows' team. As soon as I had anything close to the minimum number of hours required, I pestered my Lightning Squadron Boss to support my application to join. Fortunately, I was working for good people who probably saw that it was in the interest of the Lightning Wing to get rid of me! And so it was in the early winter of 1985 that I made my way off the Wolds and journeyed the short distance to Scampton. I had been one of the lucky few out of the 40-50 who had applied to get on to the shortlist, but because of a long-standing squadron deployment, I found myself there a week earlier than all the other candidates. So for two days I found myself as the only visitor in the Team's hallowed headquarters. Those two days were to change me forever.

I thought I wanted to be an aerobatic display pilot. I thought that given the right training I could, God willing, become good enough to be a part of one of the tightest knit and elite units within the RAF. Nothing though prepared me for the flying that was to follow.

The pre-flight briefings were all in a language that I could barely understand. I spoke fluent 'air force' but this was all new to me. Towards the end of each briefing period, sitting out of the spotlight at the back of the room, I would look at my watch and try and work out just how on Earth we were going to get from the briefing room, sign for the aeroplanes, and strap-in during the remaining few minutes. Rule One was quickly discovered; have a pee before the brief, there sure as hell isn't time afterwards. The pace from the Squadron building to the flight line was best described as brisk, and each time the Boss checked everyone in on the radio there was a full house. I was still catching my breath in the backseat.

Each sortie was a revelation. I watched in dumbstruck amazement from the back seat of a different Team pilot's aircraft each time, and got a completely different perspective of the same display routine. The speed of the formation join-ups, the slick and blindingly fast formation changes, the noise on the radio, left me reeling and wondering if the debrief would clear up any of my million and one questions. At the time I didn't feel confident enough to ask for fear of sounding completely stupid.

The ride amongst the main formation was great fun, but the real adrenaline rush, the biggest thrill of all, was riding with the two opposing solos known as the Synchro Pair. The whole experience left me exhausted, exhilarated and for once at a complete loss for words. Absolutely brilliant was all I could muster under my strained breath as I watched Scampton's rock hard runway out of the top of the canopy just a hundred feet away, having narrowly missed the other psychopathic idiot who was racing towards us at a closing speed of nearly 800 miles per hour. If I am perfectly honest, I was also a little scared, but reassured myself that these guys were handpicked and very competent. They hadn't crashed yet so why worry now — sit back and enjoy the ride!

I also discovered that the Lightning, with its size, swept wings and cluttered armoured windscreen and heavy canopy,

Opposite:
Synchro Leader Dave Stobie — 'In your face'

was a warm comfortable place to work in comparison to the nifty little Hawk. The lightly-skinned greenhouse that the Hawk sported for a canopy made me feel very exposed, like sitting on top of the aeroplane in a plastic bubble. In addition, I knew that the Lightning could not be flown this close to the ground with the same nose-down attitude and miss Mother Earth, as the graceful Hawks seemed to do with absolute impunity. Still having the aircraft's nose buried towards the centre of the airfield at a thousand feet whilst in close formation made me realise the huge difference in performance between our front-line mounts and this delightful trainer.

Back home with my wife Karen, I tried to tell her everything that had gone on. As a former WRAF officer Karen had by now developed the knack of all long-suffering Air Force wives of giving the impression of listening to their husband's rambling nonsense about aeroplanes, whilst being able to do a multitude of other things at the same time. All the same, after all the excitement of the previous two days, I now knew there was only one flying appointment in the RAF that I was prepared to trade anything for; I had to join the 'Red Arrows'.

In 1985 it wasn't to be, but the following year, having again managed to make the shortlist, I had happier news. The Friday at the end of the selection week, having just made it back to Binbrook from Scampton, the Station Commander called me at home and ordered me back to the bar in the Officers' Mess. He met me as I entered the bar, thrust a foaming pint of Bateman's

best bitter into my hand and congratulated me on somehow managing to pull the wool over everybody's eyes at Scampton. I was one of the three lucky guys that year to be accepted.

The rest of the evening was a bit of a blur, but after managing to call home and let Karen know that I was going to be a bit late, I bought a barrel of beer for the assembled masses and set about celebrating my good fortune in true RAF tradition.

In the 'Reds'

As the 1986 display season was drawing to a close, me and my fellow FNGs (Flippin' New Guys — the polite version) spent the final months flying in the Team's back seats during displays, trying to soak up as many good tips and as much advice as possible.

Although we had officially been posted on to the squadron's strength, we were not yet a part of the Team. On the stroke of Midnight on 4 October 1986, at the annual 'End of Season Guest Night' to celebrate the successful conclusion of yet another season, three team members left, and I and my fellow new boys officially became 'Red Arrows'. From here on we would be known more frequently by our allocated formation number than by name. The evening is still fresh in my memory. The assembled mass of aviation personalities and former Team pilots, and the unusually large gathering of former Team leaders, made for a spectacular gathering. I was acutely aware of being the youngest and least experienced

Above:
It's not over till it's over — even the trip back to the ramp is carefully choreographed
Opposite:
Rivets and jet pipes — when you're selected for the Team you can expect three years of a view like this!

person present, but the camaraderie of all those present made me feel that I was becoming part of aviation history.

Sunday after the guest night was a blur, but early on Monday morning the training for the '87 season began with a vengeance. With the rest of the Team taking a well-earned rest, the Boss and our group of three FNGs began the routine that became the norm throughout the winter training. Three practices a day, five days a week. Each sortie lasting just 30 minutes, but at the end of most of them you were sweaty and tired after a very physical fight to keep the aeroplane in exactly the right piece of sky.

The first sortie was quite memorable. Its aim was to get us all round our first loop and roll. Richie Thomas, then in his third and final year as leader, explained what was involved and what was expected. 'Formation aerobatics is really very simple, you have to get in the right place and stay there — any questions?'

The flying was a great challenge and the learning curve was steep, very steep. As soon as we had the basics squared away, we moved on to more complex and challenging manoeuvres. The Hawk became like a comfortable old boot; familiar and reassuring, and thanks to its rugged reliability allowed us to concentrate on the fight outside the cockpit, in the knowledge that she would take any punishment meted

Opposite:
Flt Lt Dave Stobie – 'Stobes' – dismounting from front cockpit – the physical and mental demands of synchro can be telling – especially for the third time that day

Right:
'Red over Blue'

out and never complain.

The first half of the show was formation aerobatics with all nine aircraft staying together, flying to the strains of Mozart and Beethoven. The second half of the show was pure rock and roll. The Synchro Pair would split away from the main formation and operate semi-autonomously, whilst the seven remaining aircraft of the main section set about a number of set pieces that were choreographed between the Synchro Pair's head long jousts at one another down the display line.

The training for the set pieces wasn't like anything I had ever experienced before. As Red 8, I was generally way down the back of any long line-astern manoeuvres, and the movement on a bumpy day almost defies description. The power required to stay on board almost defeated the venerable old Rolls-Royce Adour turbofan at times and called for all kind of tricks to stand

half a chance of being anywhere near the rest of the boys at the end of any manoeuvre. The airbrake would be constantly in play, against which the engine would be spooled up normally to full power, therefore minimising any acceleration time. The sight of other airbrakes coming out all down the line was not uncommon. Eventually, you learned to ignore the airbrake normally stuck right in your face from the guy a few feet in front, even when at times it seemed hell bent on getting into the cockpit with you and ruining your whole day. Another necessary ruse, was to sit as short as possible by sliding right up under the belly of the chap you were directly following, knowing that as the formation rolled out of any turns, the lag down the line would send you long, whatever you tried to do to stop it.

There were days during that winter, when it began to feel

Above:
A pilot's best briefing aid — using the hands to show what's required (but never, ever, in the pub)
Opposite:
The Synchro Pair part company from close line astern

Left:
Easing through the vertical, XX307 tucks in on Red 2
Opposite:
The team drifting onto their backs near the apex of a loop in feathered arrow, or Fred as it is colloquially called

Opposite:
'Lining up the heads'
Right:
View of the 'Caterpillar' from No 4's cockpit over the
runway at Akrotiri. Note the Hawk's shadow cast on the smoke
Below:
Flt Lt Dicky Patounis takes 'five' between sorties, resting on his
Hawk's pitot tube

quite natural to be sitting but a few feet away from a bucking, bouncing fellow Hawk. Slowly, oh so very slowly, you actually began to relax a little.

I would like to think that I never forgot just how hard some of the initial flying was, and how on numerous occasions I was working flat out with nothing left in the bank. In the years that followed, when I became the teacher, I was always conscious that people learn at different rates, although during the selection process everything is done to ensure that the fast learners are picked as well as those with outstanding pure flying ability.

At the end of the intensive winter training cycle, battling against the challenges that a typical British winter could throw at us, it was time for three weeks in the sun. Cyprus here we come! Apart from the usual distractions associated with a Mediterranean island, Cyprus offered us unrestricted flying, in beautiful skies and with a breathtaking backdrop. The show really began to 'click' and formation flying became as much a part of life's routine as getting up in the morning. On this tranquil island, the final polish was applied before our commanders watched the show to ensure we had reached the required standard before being cut loose on an unsuspecting public.

Opposite above:
Akrotiri's southern cliffs are the regular haunt of the Synchro Pair. Nestling against the rockface, and just a few feet above the ocean, 'Stobes', Synchro Lead, positions for an opposition pass
Opposite below:
Flt Lt Ian Smith, fully attired in the fabled red suit, prepares to spool up the engine of his Hawk prior to a practice sortie
Right:
'Vertical split'

In the Spotlight

My first ever public display was for some celebration or other at Jersey airport in front of the then recently married Duke and Duchess of York. It was a beautiful day and although I can now look back over 600 public displays, this one was special and the pre-match nerves were much in evidence.

We arrived over the airfield to start the show in traditional Big 9 formation with me on the extreme right. On the first change during the arrival loop into diamond, I mis-timed the power and airbrake and drifted long off the back. I could have died. The rest of the display seemed to go all right, but I was mortified at, what was in my eyes, a glaring mistake. I thought

about handing in my wings there and then, and certainly wasn't looking forward to the video debrief.

Upon hearing my confession, Richie Thomas was his usual calm unflappable self and quickly reassured me. 'Don't worry JR, these things happen', was his laconic advice; I never saw Richie ruffled, even when the going did get unusually tough.

My first year was great fun and memorable for all the right reasons. At the end of '87 I had flown 117 public displays all over Europe and was lucky enough to be selected to join Ade Thurley as a member of the Synchro Pair for the following two seasons — the best flying in the World was about to get even better.

The training for Synchro soon started in earnest and Ade Thurley was to prove one of the great teachers. He was a thoroughly professional leader, extremely able display pilot, and a good friend to boot — I was in the best possible hands. The first few sorties sapped every last drop of spare mental capacity — trying to fly the aeroplane close to the ground with the accuracy required, watch Ade's aeroplane as it zipped past my ear, put in the wind corrections, and think of all the new intricacies of this form of flying. How could Ade fly his aeroplane, lead with such precision, and effectively think for me as well? It was at times very frustrating and very humbling.

Once during the Synchro training, when the crossover point from one particular manoeuvre was consistently happening too far from crowd-centre, a very calm voice broke into my sweaty, steamy, profanity-filled cockpit with words of advice. Having just pulled 7Gs into the vertical, snap rolled through 180 degrees, pulled hard to make my gate height inverted, and preparing to pull through to race back across the airfield at Ade, the master's voice reminded me 'Don't forget the wind, JR'. Shit, yes it's my wind correction, bloody idiot Rands! Come on now push, push hard you weakling, I admonished myself, trying to keep the aircraft's nose from dropping whilst counting in the wind correction 'a thousand and one, a thousand and two', off we go, let's see if this works.

Opposite:
*Sliding up the scale towards 8'G', a single Hawk
describes its flightpath with red smoke and
wingtip vortices*
Right:
Splitting the Atmosphere

After a while the flying became more instinctive and as more practice was heaped upon more practice, the various manoeuvres began to take shape. The opposition barrel roll was quickly mastered, but more time was needed to perfect such old favourites as the double rolls and the opposition loop. What many people wouldn't consider, is the requirement to put in a correction for the fact that most spectators are looking up into the crosses, so the closer man has to put in a minor height correction — or as it is known in the trade, fudge.

Under an Angry Sky

The Synchro training for the 1988 season was really starting to look good when disaster struck the Team, and started a chain of events that was to leave us battered and bruised by the end of the summer. Ade and I had just completed an early morning training sortie and were settling down to debrief in front of the video monitor, when the airfield crash alarm sounded. Anyone who has ever heard the spine-chilling howl of the crash alarm will never forget it. Knowing that the main section were training in the overhead, it was with a sense of foreboding that we joined the gathering crowd in front of the squadron hangar and followed everybody's stare out to the East. A few kilometres beyond the airfield's eastern boundary, the sky appeared to be full of confetti, and in amongst it we could just make out a single parachute. The buzz going around was that there had been a mid-air collision and that two jets had gone down. Our worries at seeing only a single parachute only heightened our concern, and we began to fear the worst. As more facts emerged we heard that Reds 1 and 2 had somehow come to grief.

Finally, after what seemed an absolute eternity, good news was passed from the rest of the boys still airborne and now heading for the crash diversion at Waddington; they had definitely seen two chutes.

The Team's new Leader Tim Miller had been unceremoniously knocked out of the sky by one of my compatriots Spike Newbery. Poor old Spike's airbrake had failed to operate causing him to slide under Tim's tailplane as the whole formation was slowing down to reposition for the next manoeuvre. In the ensuing struggle, Spike's aeroplane wrapped itself around Tim's left wing, effectively breaking the

Above:
'Apollo' over the Island of the Gods - the team in tight formation race skyward in their Mediterranean playground
Opposite:
Somewhere over the UK a single Hawk slides into close line astern

Opposite:
*Dicky 'Pats' outlines the graphic prestart
concentration required for a sortie*
Right:
Climbing hard into the Cypriot heavens

back of Spike's aircraft, which then started to decelerate very quickly behind the rest of the formation shedding bits and pieces as it tumbled out of control. As the canopy shattered and just about all of the warning captions illuminated, Spike realised that the game was up and quickly opted to leave his doomed machine by pulling the ejection handle. As his aeroplane continued in its crazy dance towards Mother Earth, Spike's leg must have been lifted off the seat by the gyrations, and as the seat accelerated up the rails it hit one of his flailing legs with great force and broke his femur.

Tim Miller had fared little better and his predicament was getting worse by the second. Having lost its tailplane, his aircraft was now inverted and spinning quickly towards Lincolnshire's autumnal landscape. The negative 'G' forces lifted Tim against his harness and made his increasingly frantic efforts to grab the little yellow and black ejection handle between his legs more and more difficult. At the last possible moment Tim succeeded in getting to the ejection handle, and managed to leave his stricken machine around the time the performance graphs for Martin-Baker's seats began to make interesting reading.

Ade, myself, and by now most of the waterfront, were out rubbernecking and, as in most similar circumstances, feeling pretty impotent as the emergency services raced to the scene. There was nothing we could do.

We soon became bored as the show had just about run its course and headed back to the crewroom, put the kettle on, and waited for news. Within moments of arriving back inside, the telephones started their usual madness as all of the various agencies sought out the breaking news. First on the line was the Public Relations staff from our Command Headquarters hoping to put out a Press release. The question and answer session went something like this.

Command PR: 'What happened'.

JR: 'Don't know'.

Command PR: 'Who was involved'.

JR: 'Not sure'.

Command PR: 'Anybody injured'.

JR: 'Too early to say'.

At the end of many similar questions that I didn't have the answers to, and refusing to speculate having seen the damage done previously by ill-informed Press statements, I tried to be a bit more helpful with his last question.

Command PR: 'Any damage to civilian property'.

I looked out toward the East where the confetti and parachute had been, and felt sure that the ground track was well away

Above:
Briefing – it's never too dark to be cool
Opposite:
The Red's signature 'Diamond Nine' over a brilliant blue sea. Such scenes look idyllic, however the 'white horses' on the surface of the water give away the days turbulent conditions and how hard the Team are working to look this good!

from any centres of population.

JR: 'I think you should be okay on that one' I proffered.

At this point he muttered some ill-felt thanks and raced off to prepare his scoop. Little did we all realise that Spike's aeroplane had settled onto the outskirts of Welton, one of the local villages, and demolished the back of a house, missing the occupant by barely a few feet.

The poor chap, who coincidentally worked on the base, was about to step into his bath, when there was an almighty bang, his back wall disappeared in a cloud of brick dust leaving him peering out at the Lincolnshire countryside. The cartoon in the *Sun* newspaper the next day captured the poor man's ordeal in unflattering detail.

For those of us left uninjured on the Team, we set about licking our collective wounds, gave thanks that our two buddies were still around to tell the tale, and, just as importantly, that nobody else had been hurt. We didn't know it at the time, but we were to face far greater tragedy in the coming months.

The weekend following the mid-air collision, the Team were invited to join the parishioners of Welton in a thanksgiving service and I was moved by the warmth and sincerity of the welcome, knowing that feelings were running high and a vocal minority didn't want the 'Red Arrows' on their doorstep.

A few weeks later my milkman recounted how he had been delivering milk in Welton and had actually been in the infamous road at the time. He had heard the bang overhead, and watched the jet spin into the house. It brought it

Left:
'Leader's Benefit' – sitting proud out the front, the team leader with his posse low over the local scrub
Opposite above:
'Diamond Nine' over England's green and pleasant land
Opposite below:
Heading for the heavens, a single Hawk pulls hard, producing 'overwing fluff' as the wing-tip vortices tear moisture from the air

home to me that although for the Team it was a major disaster, it could have been a whole lot worse.

We set about the task of rebuilding the Team structure and individual's confidence. The scars from our first mishap had barely started to heal when late one January afternoon an accident over the airfield robbed us of Neil 'Clachy' Maclachlan, one of our Team pilots, a personal friend, and one of life's great characters. Fate could not have dealt us a crueller blow.

Again Ade and I had just finished our first sortie of the day, which had been delayed whilst the runway and taxiways were cleared of snow. The sun was now shining, and for some inexplicable reason we decided to go to the visual control room in Air Traffic Control and watch the rest of the boys practice. Everything was going well for the first half of the practice, as Ade and I settled down for a cup of tea and some friendly banter with our friends in the tower. What happened next will remain etched into my memory forever. The Team were flying over the airfield rehearsing the Roll Back manoeuvre, when Neil's aircraft departed from controlled flight and impacted the ground with tragic consequences.

Over the years I have lost many good friends in aeroplane accidents. As an RAF pilot I am not unusual. I guess we became hardened to this dark side of our profession, and use tried and tested ways of dealing with the loss. Inevitably the squadron retires to the bar and drinks away the initial shock on the recently departed member's bar book. This may seem callous, but it ensures that nobody

is left out, and most of us would prefer our friends to have one last drink on us if the worst came to the worst. The Mess always writes off a fallen member's final bill.

The 1988 display season will be remembered for all the wrong reasons. By mid-summer, we had been further reduced to flying with just seven aircraft, after Pete Collins was forced to eject on take-off from Scampton. Thankfully, he survived the incident but was declared medically unfit with a damaged back. As we set about modifying our display with two aircraft missing, the biggest ever air show disaster happened at Ramstein in Germany. Our close friends the 'Frecce Tricolori' had a mid-air collision involving three of their aircraft, one of which crashed into the crowd killing over 70 people.

Although we regularly supported the Ramstein show, in 1988 we were displaying on the south coast of England and heard the dreadful news in the early evening. The enormity of the tragedy took some time to sink in. The following morning whilst we prepared for a show at Exeter, some chap whom we had never previously met appeared with a TV crew in tow and announced that he was going to give us a safety brief. Apparently, he had

Opposite:
Looking down on the Team's borrowed
dispersal area in Cyprus through line
abreast. Rolling inverted over the
Akrotiri runway in line abreast,
it looks easy – it isn't
Right:
Easing away

some tenuous link with the air show we were supporting and believed it would be good PR for his display if he was seen to be laying the law down to us about flight safety. Air show briefings are usually very comprehensive and attended by all participants, and the snub this chap wanted to deliver was quickly seen off by Cub Carter, who left him in no doubt as to his place in the proceedings. The Press hounded us for a few days with all the usual questions in their search for instant answers. Yes we knew the 'Frecce' well, no we didn't know what happened, yes flight and crowd safety are our prime concerns, no we aren't planning any immediate changes, etc, etc. The political aftershocks of the Ramstein tragedy were to hound the Team for many years to come.

I was pleased when the 1988 season closed. Frankly I had had enough. At times it was difficult to imagine things

Above:
The school bullies safely airborne as Red 7 slides into the box,
prior to the nine-ship join-up
Left:
A single Hawk slides in to inverted port echelon – inverted
Right:
Looking through the back end of the formation, tucking in for the run-in

returning to normal — the sense of gloom was endemic.

They say that only in the darkest hours do the real leaders appear and part of our salvation lay in Tim Miller's unswerving belief in his team, and his unstinting desire to rebuild and return us to our former glory. At the time Tim was injured with post-ejection injuries to his back, and had to spend three months recuperating on the ground. Everyone expected Tim to climb straight back into an aeroplane and get stuck into training the Team again as soon as his injuries would allow. The fact that he had very nearly been killed, and had witnessed 'Clachy's' accident, never occurred to anyone at the time. Looking back, I marvel at Tim's immense inner strength and courage. It was one of life's great lessons, Tim Miller was made of 'the right stuff'.

Opposite above:
The left side go 'flat' in 'Big Nine' just prior to running in to start the show

Opposite below:
Runway beat-up — by Spike Jepson 'down in the weeds'

Right:
Line Abreast

A letter from one of our former members also helped. It was full of encouragement, and told how from a previous season many years before the Team had been through similarly dark days, but with faith in our own abilities things would get better. I met the said gentleman at our end of season guest night and thanked him for his support. I told him how we felt we were letting our illustrious forebears down, but again he was very supportive, 'Don't worry son, we've all been there, keep your chin up and next year will be fine'. He was right. Out of the ashes of '88 came a brilliant '89. It was the last year of my tour, but what a year it was!

Synchro Training
Thus it was, that after struggling with the intricacies of missing Ade (he had already finished his tour), talking on the radio, and being able to count up to five all at the same time (!), I had the honour of training my own Synchro wingman, Steve 'Jos' Johnson. Jos and I had joined the RAF on the same day and been on the same training squadrons throughout basic, advanced and weapon training before going to different

frontline aircraft. He was the godfather of one of my sons and had been the best man at my wedding several years before. Now we were flying together again, and 'old banana hands' Johnson was an impressive aviator to train. We had only one agreement and that was that we would still be around to talk about it at the end of the season, i.e. no heroics! On top of this, Jos had the 'Synchro Brick' as an extra insurance policy. This common house brick was handed down to successive Synchro pilots; the idea being that if everything was slipping away, and you didn't have enough height to complete a pull out from a manoeuvre, you only had to open the canopy and throw out the brick, lighten the load and thus theoretically guarantee survival. The brick, with its cheap label, normally sits as a badge of office on the Synchro wingman's desk throughout his year as Red 7.

Towards the end of the winter training period, and before the display routine for the forthcoming season was finalised, Jos was champing at the bit to try a bit of inverted close formation. The commonly held belief was that the Hawk, for all of its carefree handling, wasn't the right machine for an inverted routine, and to date none had been attempted. With the blessing from the hierarchy, we set about improving our own inverted flying skills before getting too close together, whilst Jos spent many an interesting moment practising the roll in and out of the inverted a few feet above my tailplane, while I towed for him the right way up.

Eventually we could both hold a pretty good inverted line, discovering how much easier the manoeuvre was at 150ft than at 500ft, the horizon being that much easier to judge. When I look back at the halcyon season that was the summer of '89, the Synchro inverted run is one of my proudest memories. Jos, as Synchro Leader the following year, refined the manoeuvre further and today the Synchro Pair use a much improved and more spectacular version.

Above:
Follow the Leader, 'Enid' fan into the vertical at the start of the 'Caterpillar'
Right:
Synchro take a breather from their low level jousting

From the Cockpit

The Hawk is a delight to fly and very simple to operate. Its systems are simple, robust and very reliable — in fact during my first three-year tour with the 'Reds', I don't remember ever having to climb out of an aeroplane because of unserviceability.

It takes but a few seconds to board and strap into the excellent Martin-Baker ejection seat, before literally flicking a few switches and firing up the remarkable Rolls-Royce Adour turbofan engine which breathes life into this Hawker-Siddeley masterpiece. The airframe/engine combination is a mechanical marriage made in heaven, proving totally reliable and as tough as old boots. The punishment meted out during just a single Synchro practice, is testament to the Hawk's incredible inner strength.

The Hawks flown by the Team are from the first production batch of aircraft delivered to the RAF. The cockpit is very traditional, with none of the fancy glass screens and state-of-the-art avionics that adorn the export version today. The seat, apart from being very comfortable, has been proven in the most extreme circumstances, and the view from both seats is exceptional.

The beauty of this aeroplane for the aerobatic display pilot is the knowledge that the aircraft will literally look after itself, allowing the pilot to concentrate outside the cockpit where all of the action is.

Take-off in formation is straightforward and uncomplicated, with the rudder becoming effective at about 50kts, and the lift-off achieved between 120-130kts depending on aircraft weight. The Team's engines have a modified fuel control system that allows faster acceleration and deceleration of the Adour turbofan.

Turbofans give greater fuel economy than turbojets (great news for a trainer), but are generally slower to wind up and down (not so good for aerobatics). However, with the 'mod', from brakes release the Team can get airborne, join-up, accelerate to standard operating speeds and be back over display centre pulling up into the first loop, in just three minutes.

Learning to be a Wingman

Flying close formation is 'bread and butter' to most RAF pilots. The need to formate on take-off and landing is an everyday requirement on the front-line, and all aircrew are trained accordingly. Formation aerobatics isn't taught, nor is it allowed in everyday operations. So, although a pilot that joins the 'Red Arrows' may have 10 years military flying experience behind him and be the best bomber or fighter pilot around, he hasn't any experience of what will be required for the next three years. Everything has to be taught from scratch.

The one human quality that cannot be discovered from

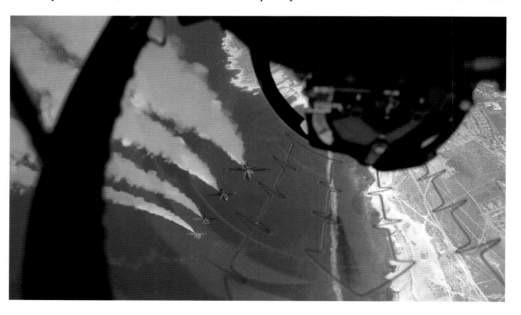

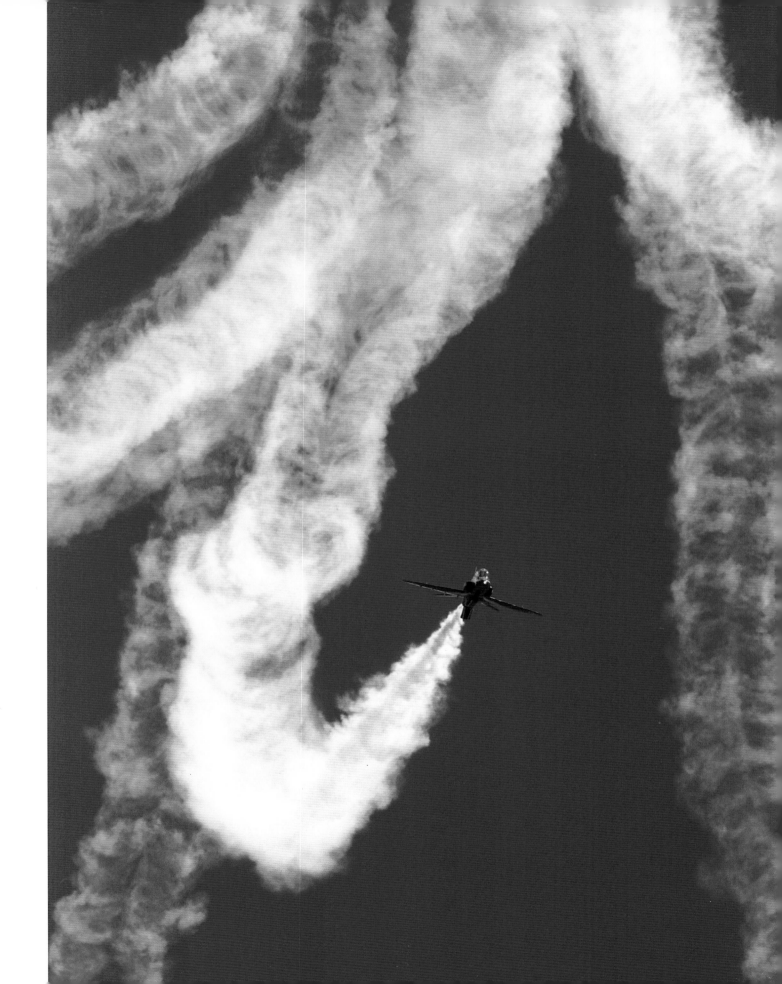

Opposite:
On the downswing of the 'Caterpillar' viewed from Five's cockpit. Four's airbrake is already out as everyone juggles power and drag to maintain the spacing

Right:
When the day is nearly done – at the bottom of the 'Spaghetti' one aircraft pulls hard to dump speed as it heads for the landing pattern at the end of another show with 7 'G' on the meter

reading training reports, or from liaising with a candidate's squadron hierarchy, is that of tenacity in the face of adversity. Sure, the chances are that if a guy is a good aggressive combat pilot and low-level leader, he will have the necessary bottle, but flying with the 'Reds' isn't everybody's cup of tea. Some people just do not settle into the type of flying that the role demands, and there is never any shame or stigma attached to individuals who, having tried out with the Team, decide that it isn't for them. In fact I admire them the more for it.

The first few days of training are spent on the leader's wing, building confidence and learning the pitch and roll rates used in the loops and rolls. The next building block is when more aircraft are added to the formation. New pilots have to learn to be able to formate off the leader, even though there may be two or three aircraft

separating them. Although from the ground there may appear to be very little movement inside the formation, take it from me that the situation can best be described as fluid, and down right bloody scary at worse.

Occasionally the air is totally calm with hardly a zephyr to stir the windsock. On such days life can be very pleasant. The opposite end of the spectrum though is the standard blustery UK afternoon, where the wind travels in from the Atlantic to be stirred up into eddies, vortices and air pockets from the Welsh and Pennine hills. Here we discover just how uncomfortable flying close together can be, and how much the lightly loaded Hawk's wing likes to dance in the uneven air. What is already a very physical battle of concentration and will, becomes a roughhouse where physical strength can be severely tested, and individual

Opposite above:
Jet-pipe detail, clearly showing the three pipes that pump the diesel and dye into the jet efflux to create the famous coloured smoke
Opposite below:
Streamers off the wingtip as 'Gypo' start to 'rock and roll' at the start of the 'Corkscrew'
Right:
'Diamond Nine' looping over the bay

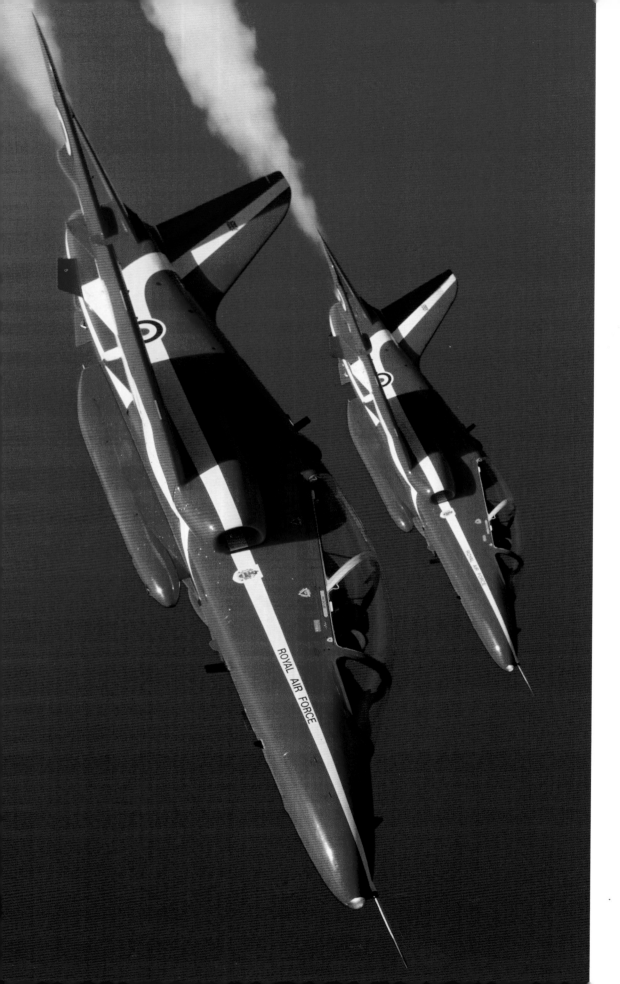

nerves can become frayed.

The standard UK winter is a great test for *ab-initio* display pilots, with the Lincoln Edge upon which Scampton perches giving the already violent airflow an added bit of uplift and energy. I vividly remember my first winter work-up. The strong North-Westerlies seemed to blow for weeks on end and our first exposure to them was a baptism of fire. The Boss at the time, Richie Thomas, briefed us that the going would be tough, and that we must try to damp out the bigger bumps and work really hard to stay in our allotted piece of sky. On the rougher days the turbulence could be totally fatiguing, and no matter how tightly I pulled the lap straps to anchor me more firmly into the seat, the turbulence always seemed to dislodge me and make the ride akin to racing over cobblestones on solid tyres.

Like everything else, with training and near constant exposure to the winter winds, we learned to ride with the bumps and relax a little. The problem now was always on the first calm day when we would all generally fly so tight to give us the same workload. Sitting in the right position without the buffeting wind seemed far too easy, and gave a sense that you were out of position, sitting too far out in the calmer air.

Even with the better engines, the acceleration times were still too slow for a lot of the moves and manoeuvres. In training, and even on the front-line, the use of airbrake when other aircraft were in close line astern was forbidden. The fear being that if the trailing aircraft didn't see the airbrake going out, or

Opposite:
Reds two-ship pour on the bank
Above
*Racing in over the coast – a pair of Reds scurry
in for the join up*
Right:
*Condensation streaming off the wingtips as this
singleton Hawk pulls away with streamers –
synchro piles on the 'G' round the bend*

missed the radio call, the ensuing bunching up could be catastrophic. In the 'Reds' the airbrake was an essential tool that anybody apart from the Boss could use at any time. The trick was to anticipate any imminent position changes by powering up against the airbrake, so, when needed, the engine was already producing close to full power, and by flicking the airbrake in you could quickly move forward. So it was that you very quickly came to ignore the large ventral airbrake belonging to the guy in front.

The other big lesson to be learned early on in training is when to start pulling up into a loop or roll. If you waited for the aircraft in front or beside you to move first, then there would be an increasing delay the further away you were from the leader, leading to problems at the extremity of the formation. When the Boss called 'pulling up' or 'and rolling', you had to react. The secret is for the whole formation to pitch together, which takes total trust in the Boss and those others around you. Like learning to fly quite a distance from the leader while still

formating on his aircraft, getting used to the cadence in the Boss' voice, and exactly when he puts in an input as he talks on the radio, comes with continual practice. As I would discover during my own time in command, consistency is the basis for success.

The average UK winter is a hotchpotch of wind, rain, sleet, snow, weeks of fog, and the occasional crisp blue day. We always flew if there was only even half a chance of finding some usable airspace, and I mean always. Sometimes for weeks on end we could only practice the flat manoeuvres that could be completed under a low cloudbase, and dreamed of clearer weather to enable us to go 'full', i.e. have room to loop. By the end of March we would have flown our first nine-ship display, and worked hard to perfect the following year's sequence. What was lacking was consistency that comes from continual hard practice. Hence the yearly push to Cyprus to put on the finishing touches and polish. Cyprus is absolutely perfect for formation aerobatic training.

Opposite:
Harvest season – the famous nine transit through an autumnal England
Right:
High above the saltlake and against a dazzling skyscape – the Team cascade in 'Feathered Arrow'

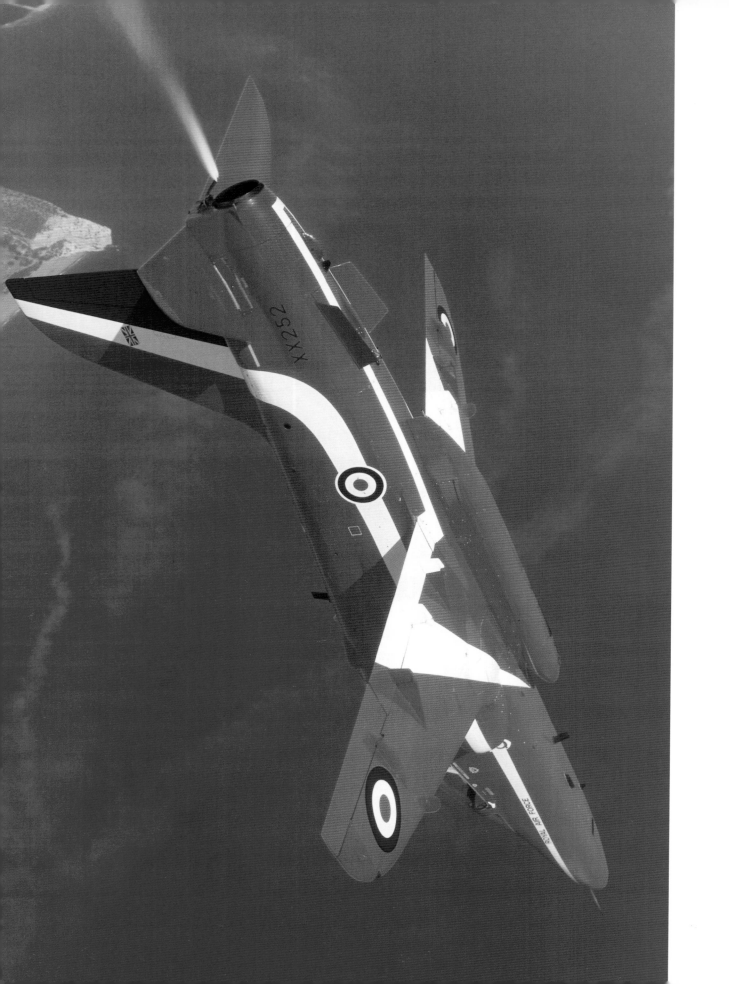

By April the worst aspects of the Mediterranean winter are over. The air is mostly clear, the sun shines and the Team can take full advantage of the excellent display venues in the local area. The airfield at Akrotiri sits on a small peninsular on the southern part of the island. The airspace is uncluttered, the runway long and wide, and the local cliffs and harbour area are fairly representative of many of the venues to be visited throughout the summer.

Up to this point, all of the training has taken place over land, and for the Team's new recruits this will be the first time they have trained over the sea, which brings with it a number of potential pitfalls. Overland, height can be fairly accurately judged by

Above:
Mirror image. Tim Couston and Kelvin Truss
were the Synchro duo for the 1996 season.
Right:
Easing astern chased by his own fading red
smoke, Andy Cubin rolls and pushes during the
'synchro'
Opposite:
Shame it wasn't Apollo! The 'Reds' chase their
shadows as 'Big Vixen' is eased down over
a saltlake 'moonscape'

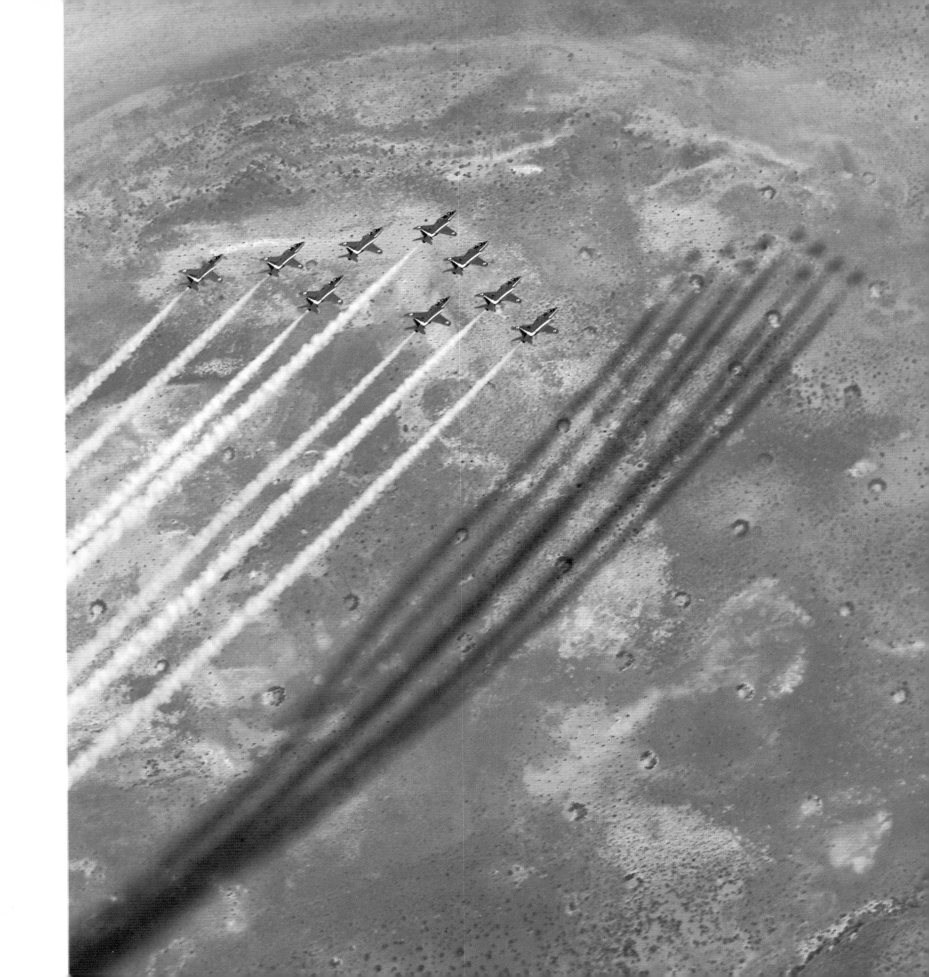

reference to ground features, and the contrasting landscape helps you easily differentiate between land and sky.

In stark contrast, the sea can offer very little help in maintaining spatial awareness, and the aircraft's instruments are used far more than over land. Depth perception and visual height assessment can become very unreliable. During the times when high pressure regions dominate our UK summers, the haze and general poor visibility can make flying away from the coast very disorientating — not too far removed from flying in thick custard.

By the end of the 3-4 week deployment in Cyprus, the Team will be comfortable over any location, and probably have practised over a few of the local seafronts along the South Cypriot coast as well.

The journey out to Cyprus normally takes in a night-stop in Rivolto, Northern Italy, the home of our long-standing friends the 'Frecce Tricolori'. Here we get together over a meal and a few glasses of the local wine (Rivolto sits surrounded by vineyards — now there's style) to exchange ideas and catch up with the latest buzz in this part of Europe. The 'Reds' have excellent working relationships with all the European teams from many air forces, but my admiration for the Italians has only increased over the 10 years I was privileged to have worked alongside them.

Opposite left:
On the ground as in the air — perfect formation
Opposite lower:
Over a solid undercast, one of the boys hangs on
inverted a few feet off the photographer's wing
Right:
Looping 'D-9'

Above:
*Arching over the Med —
Leader Simon Meade brings
the Team round as viewed
from Red 5*

Right:
*'Last drink before bedding
down for the night' – at the end
of a long day, one of the Team's
Hawks has its tanks topped off
with fuel. Tomorrow it all
happens again*

Right:
*Climbing through 4,000ft, John
Rands leads a welded
formation over the coast*

Red Leader

At the end of '89, my three-year tour with the Team was over, and new challenges lay ahead. I was very lucky to be allowed to transfer away from Air Defence duties and join the cloistered world of the Mud Movers, as the RAF Ground Attack fraternity are known.

I was posted to fly the Vertical Take Off and Landing Harrier, but before I could get my hands on the real thing I had to complete six hours of helicopter flying, trying to get to grips with hovering. Helicopter flying is one of the best kept secrets around, and the week spent at RAF Shawbury flying the little Gazelle was outrageous fun and deeply satisfying.

Soon afterwards I was at RAF Wittering, home of the Harrier Conversion Unit, beginning yet another aviation love affair. The Harrier is, and always will be, one of the great aviation success stories. I learned initially on the older T4 and GR3 aircraft, before finally getting my hands on the magnificent GR5. For three wonderful years I served on No. 3 (F) Squadron

in Germany, and had an absolute ball. The Squadron deployed all over Europe, as well as the USA, Greece and finally Turkey. The Squadron eventually re-equipped with the GR7, which allowed the Harrier force to specialise in night operations using the electro-optical devices that came free with every aeroplane.

But, once again, the allure of the 'Arrows' was never far away.

During my stay in Germany the rumour factory had been working overtime, and the word on the street was that the new 'Red Arrows' Team leader would be announced imminently. As in all good rumours, the timing was well out and it was to be a few months later that those of us who had previously flown on the Team and aspired to go back and lead would be put out of our collective misery. I knew that my flying training records had disappeared from the Squadron, and that I was being assessed for what I considered to be the best flying appointment the RAF had to offer . . . but there was tough competition.

I had not always felt this way about being in charge of the 'Reds'. In fact I had been lukewarm to the idea when, on leaving the Team in 1989, I was told that the odds for coming back to Scampton to lead the Team were pretty good. After flying with the Synchro for two years I could not imagine any flying competing with the pure adrenaline rush that epitomised low-level opposition aerobatics. I argued that I had probably seen all there was to see, and sitting at the front of the formation was very restrictive in actually flying the aeroplane — and the responsibility that went with the job overawed me more than a little.

Over the intervening four years I had chance to reflect on my earlier misgivings

Opposite:
To have any chance of staying aboard in 'Big Nine' prior to running in to start the show, the chaps on the port wing go into a flat turn
Right:
Tim Couston slices through the English Summer skies

and now was desperately keen to succeed my old Synchro partner Ade Thurley, who was currently filling the slot.

The decision when it was made took me, and many others, completely by surprise. I had just finished a day away in the UK from my base at Gutersloh in Germany, and after three very pleasurable sorties around the wonderful UK low-level system, had retired to the bar in the Officers' mess at RAF Leuchars. I was barely into my first pint of Heavy (which is a Scottish substitute for beer), when a Tannoy message called me to the phone in reception. The voice at the other end of the line announced she was the ADC to the Commandant of the Central Flying School, and that I should stand by while she connected me. Air Commodore Gordon McRobbie quickly came on the line and introduced himself and then announced that I

Opposite above:
A single Red curves across a soft drifting cumulus
backdrop — summer '98
Opposite below:
The Boss — Simon Meade prebriefs every single
sortie, generally using one of the Hawk's wings as
a makeshift desk
Right:
Plunging from the Heavens — this gives a sense
of the amount of sky a jet aerobatic team can get
through during a 'full' show

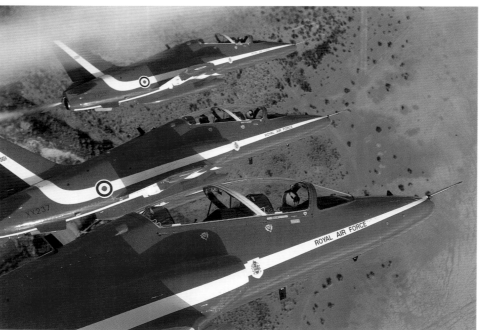

had been selected from a cast of four to lead the Team from the end of 1993. I was then, and remain to this day, the luckiest chap in the RAF.

The hangover, when I sobered up sufficiently to realise I had one, was an absolute beauty.

After my selection, I had another 18 months in Germany trying to keep a clean slate before moving back to the UK, but the wait was worth it. Shortly before leaving No. 3 (F) Squadron, Ade Thurley rang to ask if I was interested in flying the spare aircraft around America at the end of the '93 season, if the planned USA tour came off. It took me all of a few milliseconds to agree, and start praying that the 'powers that be' agreed to the Tour.

In September 1993 I completed a short

Above:
Against an azure blue Mediterranean, the 'Red Arrows'
inverted in 'Apollo' formation
Left:
The Team races across the Cypriot wilderness

Above:
*Hanging on in there! The view from down the
back of long line astern*

Left:
A beautiful saltlake backdrop frames
this singleton 'Red Arrows' Hawk
Opposite above:
'Cubes' in cockpit — using the pre-start
calm to reflect on what's to come
Opposite below:
The classic 'Reds' scheme – utilising the
Hawk's belly area to create a white
framed red arrow

refresher course on the Hawk at RAF Valley before joining Ade and his Team mid-way through the month. The USA tour started the day after the Team had completed two displays, and barely pausing to catch breath we set off across the great expanse of the North Atlantic to start five weeks of outstanding aviation, and unbridled American hospitality.

This was to be a truly great way to get back into the swing of all things 'Red Arrows'. In the four years I had been away, there had been subtle changes in the way the Team went about its business, and I tried to soak up everything I could. The tour of the States was a great success, and a fitting way for Ade to see out his time in command. Seeing most of the USA from the air was tremendous. In five weeks, we traversed from our landfall in Canada, across to

the West Coast via Denver, down through Arizona, back across the Southern states, to Dallas and New Orleans, before tracking up the East Coast to head back across the now winter bound North Atlantic and home.

Throughout this time, I hung onto the Team's coat-tails, became the unofficial photographer, and had a thoroughly wonderful time.

The '93 Team gave its final display in Ottawa on a blustery and chilly afternoon. I was very impressed by the standard that the boys had maintained thoughout the five weeks I was with them. Secretly I felt very proud at being allowed back into this close-knit world and, if I was truthful, just a little daunted by what lay ahead over the coming months.

Before I could officially take over the reigns from Ade, we had to get 11 Hawks and all of the Team support back across the North Atlantic. In just five weeks, the clear blue summer skies that had accompanied us on our Western trail were nowhere to be seen, and the water of the North Atlantic looked grey and menacing.

Leaving Goose Bay in Newfoundland for the long sea crossing, I, and all fellow Hawk crew, were dressed in the best survival gear that the RAF is famous for. Coated in layer upon layer of thermal underclothing, and cocooned in a one piece immersion suit, we all looked like complete fat boys as we waddled out to our waiting aircraft in the frosty half light of dawn. Already

Opposite:
'Leader rolling under now...' starting the 'Twizzle'
Above:
The Hawk's punchy performance is to a degree masked by its smooth, passive lines —
'Offo' and 'Stobes' captured on a cumulus rooftop

it was shockingly cold, with few people hanging about outside their aircraft before smartly jumping aboard and closing the lid.

The two and a bit hours to Greenland was as boring as all long transit sorties, and with just a grey panorama of cloud beneath, with the odd glimpse of the ocean below, the minutes dragged on. Instead of the blinding sunshine and virgin white vista of the ice plateau that greeted us on our west bound journey, Sondestrom Fjord with its airfield tucked right up in the narrow recesses 80 miles from the sea, was hidden beneath a ragged, ugly, dripping bank of stratus, embedded with granite cliff faces and razor-sharp peaks. After weeks of sunshine and humidity this was a rude welcome back to the reality of European-style weather, and the tricks it can play.

Relieved to be safely down and parked alongside Sondestrom's lonely runway, the journey home was about to be brought to an abrupt halt.

The 'Met man' hadn't forecast the cloud ceiling at our next destination in Iceland being on the surface, or the 40 plus knots of wind that was blowing across the US military airfield at Keflavik. We were stuck!

Opposite:
Keeping it tight
Right:
Looping 'Card' over a sparkling sea. Depth perception is very difficult during coastal displays and accurate instrument flying is vital

For just over three days we languished in the small Danish-run hotel alongside the airfield waiting for the weather to break. To top it all, it began to snow in Sondestrom . . . and snow. . . and snow. I made the mistake of asking one of the locals if the snow would soon be gone, to which he replied in a dead-pan manner that 'Oh yes, normally by April the snow starts to clear' - only six months to wait!

Eventually, after a number of false starts thwarted by the extreme winter temperatures, we set off early one morning into a beautiful star-filled sky. The runways and taxiways had been sufficiently cleared of snow, although there was a fine icing-sugar layer on all the hard surfaces and everyone taxied with the utmost care. It was the eerie half-light between night and day, when the Sun had not yet wrestled back

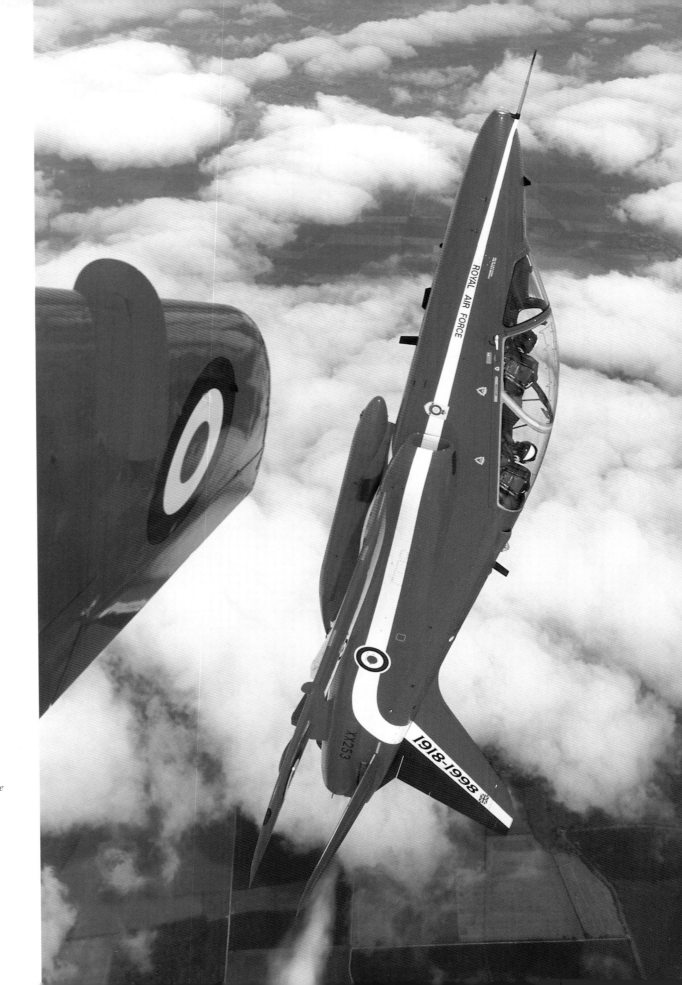

Opposite above:
The 'Office'
Opposite below:
The majesty of the heavens is the regular
playground during high manoeuvres
Right:
Showing off the artwork on the tails to celebrate
80 years of the RAF, the Team ease vertically
through the clouds in search of some sun
on the wings

the sky from the Moon, that we raced one after another into the Greenland dawn.

The air was icily cold, a good 15 degrees C below freezing, and the super-cooled air gave our dear old Hawk's engines a real kick in the pants. I guess both aeroplane and pilot were pleased to be heading in the right direction again, and the Hawk showed her appreciation by leaping into the air like a startled rabbit and then climbing like a homesick angel.

As the last man airborne, I called Ade to let him know we were all in good shape, and he replied that he was already passing 15,000ft. The group I was following were the rear section, or 'Gypo' as they are affectionately known, and they were having one final fling across a virgin lake just to the East

of the airfield. I watched their twinkling anti-collision beacons strung out across the polished mirror surface like glowing moths before we all eased the noses of our mounts skywards to join the party heading home.

Two hours later, after another journey above the stratus-shrouded ocean, we were surrounded by the spectacularly grey featureless landscape of Iceland, as we positioned to land at Keflavik and drink in more fuel for the onward journey.

Leaving Keflavik the day got even longer as, with insufficient fuel to make Scampton in a single hop, we set down on the shore of the Firth of Forth at Kinloss as the Scottish evening fell. Cold, tired and by now desperately keen to get home, we again slaked the Hawks' thirst for kerosene, and quickly set off South as the first evening stars splashed across a rapidly darkening sky.

The final leg took less than an hour, and now in small sections of twos and threes, Ade led his Team home for the final time. The Team had been away for five weeks after a long summer spent displaying across the length and breadth of Europe with the finale of the U.S. Tour.

The families were gathered, the champagne flowed in fine 'Red Arrows' tradition, and just another average sort of day came to an end. Soon, the mantle of Leader, and all the responsibilities would be mine. Ade had left big boots to fill and I was in little doubt of the challenges ahead.

Opposite above:
Synchro rolling and inverted 150ft up and 350mph on the clock!
Opposite below:
Starting the second half of the show, the Gypo four ship have just rolled and prepare for the crowd-stopping split across each other
Right:
Dicky Patounis heads for the debrief

'Smoke on . . . Go'

Everything, but everything, is run by the clock, and today is no exception. Every member of the Team, be they pilot or engineer has a copy of the itinerary or WHAM (What's Happening Manager) as it is known, and from the moment they wake, to the end of the day, everything is choreographed to the minute.

We have just spent the night in Bournemouth on England's South coast, having performed two displays and two transit sorties the previous day. Today we fly to Switzerland, refuel and display in the middle of the Swiss Alps, then later on fly to Newcastle to position for two shows in the Northeast the following day — all pretty standard stuff.

It is an 'Oh dark early' departure, so the engineers will be at the airfield pre-dawn, whilst the pilots plan to arrive with just enough time to grab a quick 'cuppa' before briefing.

I always go on the early transport with whichever pilot is looking after the navigation. The Team has no professional navigators as such, and all of the planning is shared by three of the Team pilots, and a first-class job they make of it.

In the early morning I normally try to grab a few moments to myself with the maps and display information for the coming day. Time on my own is a much valued commodity, and sitting

on the wing of my aeroplane whilst the boys busy themselves with the final aircraft preparation, is a great way to start the day. I study the weather and navigation warnings, check the timings, and ensure I have everything I need for all the day's sorties — later on there won't be enough time to catch breath, so falling behind the time line isn't an option. I also mentally go through the next brief, thinking how I am going to get 10 aircraft onto this short runway, how we are going to join-up, transit details, and most importantly, how we are going to find the airfield at the far end and how we will arrive.

With but a few minutes to spare, the Team congregates by the middle jet and starts collecting the maps they need. Some prefer to be there early, others prefer to saunter up with seconds to go. The bottom line is that when I run the time check to start the brief, everyone is there ready to go.

As is standard with big airshows, we have been allocated an exact time to arrive. This means we have to be airborne to the second, which means that briefing, start-up and taxi are all planned with the single aim of getting the 'Red Arrows' anywhere in the World at the agreed time.

Today we are heading off to Switzerland, to display in front of a large crowd, as well as all the other European display teams. To add a little extra spice, the display venue is at a place called Buochs, which is very beautiful but is surrounded by big, jagged, very very hard mountains. It is probably one of the most challenging display venues we will face this year — but we are prepared.

A few months earlier when flying out to Cyprus, we stayed with the Swiss national team, and landed at Buochs. That trip was a great adventure as the weather was pretty awful, and our experience of flying amongst Switzerland's green and pleasant land wasn't great. The redeeming feature then was the great air traffic control, which allowed us to let down at Emmen (a large airbase to the north), and then fly across a lake, nip down a mountain pass and land at this incredible wartime base tucked into the valley floor. On landing, the clouds still covered the

Opposite:
Symmetry
Right:
Smoke on the water — looping over the Med casts
a shadow of the smoke trail on the sea below

Left:
Rolling 'Flanker'
Opposite above:
The groundcrew busy themselves fuelling
and 'dieseling' the jets
Opposite below:
Line abreast bend

hills all around so we couldn't really get a feel for the topography, but the following morning in bright sunshine we stared in awe at this 'telephone booth' we would later display in.

Knowing that we were programmed to return later in the year, we managed to liberate a couple of detailed maps and later, back at Scampton, set about planning how on earth we could fit our display in this valley surrounded to the front and back with imposing hills.

The problem became apparent when we overlaid the Swiss map with one of the airspace around Scampton, and by plotting exactly where we positioned for certain manoeuvres, tried to find a way of making our routine fit.

Normally we wouldn't change our basic routine for anything. The risk of individuals who have practised consistently a set routine over many weeks being asked to do something completely different, was well known. More importantly, our display routine had been scrutinised and cleared at the highest level and, quite simply, I didn't have the authority to arbitrarily change things.

By using the few spare minutes at the end of normal practice sorties, we quickly learned that we could get most of the show in, but certain positioning turns, and some Synchro moves, needed slight modification. Armed with this knowledge, we applied for permission to modify our routine for one show only. After demonstrating that we had all the

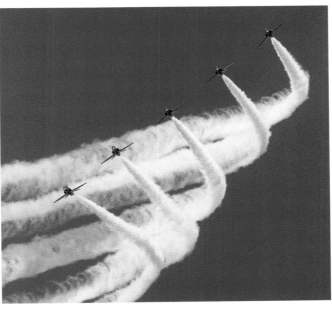

angles covered, we were granted approval.

And so it was, that I led the Team airborne along the South coast and off to a venue that would be a test of just how good our planning had been. Now normally transits are pretty boring and monotonous, and anybody who claims to enjoy flying in straight lines for hours on end needs their head examining. Today's boring transit was to be different, with an unusual snag manifesting itself in one of the aircraft's aileron controls. Unable to risk putting the aircraft into the tight mountainous airfield at Buochs, we elected to land a few miles away at Emmen, where the approach and climb-out paths weren't blocked by big hills. Although this kept us away from the main action, it all helped with the drama that was to follow.

The Swiss Team are masters of mountain flying and were totally unperturbed by the terrain, but the rest of the Teams were obviously not. I have always steadfastly played down any talk of competition amongst the Teams, but this day was a real gift. Out of sight of us, the French and Italian Teams gave only parts of their displays, or restricted themselves to a series of flypasts '. . . and for heaven's sake the Brits had to land up the valley somewhere'.

With Red 7 flying the spare aircraft, whilst the boys worked to find the control fault on his normal machine, we launched into a beautiful summer's afternoon, with the bluest sky and the most remarkable scenery. The adrenaline was on tap.

We arrived down the valley at Buochs instead of from behind the crowd as was usual, and at exactly 14.00hrs, pulled up into our first loop carrying a lot of extra speed to make up for the 1,500ft elevation, and plus 30 degree heat in the valley. Keeping the boys in diamond for a complete 360 degree bend was the real confidence builder, and allowed me to judge just how much room we had to play with. With the air so clear, and the mountains so big, it felt as if the harsh jagged peaks would rip through the cockpit floor at any time, but although they looked uncomfortably close, I knew our modified show would fit. The next 20 minutes went by too quickly. The Synchro Pair did a magnificent job, and the Team put on one of the best displays, against the most awesome backdrop I can remember.

We finished the show on a storming Vixen Break, and then disappeared just as quickly as we came, leaving only the fading notes from our engines reverberating around these timeless hills and the slowly settling streams of patriotic red, white and blue smoke dissipating in the valley's crystal air. The atmosphere on the ground was electric — I guess that by not

Opposite:
A sky full of Hawks
Right:
Screaming across a headland at low level

operating from Buochs just added to the overall affect.

Much later that evening, sitting outside the hotel bar by the River Tyne in Newcastle, I reflected on just another routine day — well, almost.

Just Like Flying a Jumbo

Although the Hawk is capable of the most remarkable feats of aerobatic manoeuvring, if you are sitting at the front of nine aeroplanes you have to fly this lively little fighter like a big lumbering Jumbo Jet.

I knew that this kind of flying would be very different, but I never thought I would get the immense satisfaction that I had when flying with Synchro — like many things in my life, I was wrong.

A good sortie starts with a good brief. Time to myself before any trip, be it a practice or public display, is vitally important. Everyone wants a piece of you, but at least 15 minutes before every brief, I would leave the office and sit in the quiet of the briefing room on my own, no phones and no pestering — absolute bliss. Like a small child I play with the magnetic aircraft shapes, all designed to look like Hawks; all red and all numbered. In the early part of the work-up, this two

dimensional squadron on the briefing board is worth its weight in best bitter. Later on it will only be used for the more unusual sorties that require something a little out of the ordinary.

Time and the stopwatch rule supreme virtually every working day. You can never give yourself too much time, and frequently you allow too little. It's just like decorating your house in terms of how long you think it will take — think of the first number that comes into your head, add a nought on the end, and then double it; briefings can run on if you let them. That said, I always tried to slow everything down during training — if a brief overran then so be it. Rushing and aeroplanes are uneasy bedfellows!

At the end of the brief would come the relevant timings, most importantly check-in. Most pilots have the short-term memory of a Goldfish, so getting them into their aeroplanes ready to start on time was the showstopper. Check-in time would be dependent on the runway in use and time required to get nine or ten aircraft along the various taxiways and lined up in time for take off. Life is much more pleasant sitting on the runway with everything in place, rather than racing around some strange airfield with the stopwatch already counting down the flying time to the display venue.

To get to any show to the second, the 'navs' will have planned very accurately on half-million scale maps for the trip from the operating airfield to the display area, then transfer onto 1:50,000 scale Ordnance Survey maps for the run-in to the site itself. The timing on the maps will be elapsed timing, allowing me to nominate the exact engine wind-up and brakes

Opposite above:
On the way to the show, the Team heads out to
the runway
Opposite below:
Red, white and blue
Right:
Looping 'Apollo' in the hall of the mountain kings
– the breathtakingly beautiful Troodos mountains
provide the distant scenery as the Team sit in
close in formation

Left:
Profile of a Thoroughbred. The Hawk's beautiful lines are shown to perfection in this stunning image of a singleton holding the vertical

Opposite:
Inch perfect — the pre-season Cyprus training pays dividends

release time on my wristwatch, then transfer to the aircraft's stopwatch for the remainder of the sortie. The stopwatch sits at eye-level on the cockpit coaming, is deadly accurate, and is what all RAF pilots are trained to use and feel comfortable with.

A typical display sortie will start with a briefing on the wing of the most central aircraft 30 minutes before take-off. The pilot responsible for 'nav' planning on this day will provide all of the maps, will have verified display timings, and liaised with all the relevant air traffic agencies. Synchro will have pre-briefed using aerial photographs of the site from the Team's extensive library, and from their Ordnance Survey pitch maps that are specially covered with display line and relevant headings. These are normally affixed in small plastic sleeves just above the attitude indicator in the cockpit for quick reference if needed during the display. I also carry a pitch map in my aircraft, and have a map storage sleeve down the side of my ejection seat; getting all the husbandry right with the various maps is a large part of the job. I keep my half-mill map always readily to hand, with my more detailed final run-in map secure under my thigh ready to pick up once I have identified the run-in Initial Point.

The briefing itself covers the type of take-off and join up, all the routes in and out of the site, and how we are going to fit our display into the topography we will be faced with, drawing corrections or minor improvements warranted by our previous display.

Having answered any questions, I reiterate the check-in time and we disburse to our individual aircraft.

Here the 'Red Arrows' are different from most RAF squadrons. Each pilot normally stays with one particular aircraft for most, if not all of the display season. The Synchro jets are particularly important, having been specially selected to take the lion's share of the fatigue burden for one season, and then be rested in less punishing positions the following year.

I remember thinking when I first joined the Team in 1986 how incredible it was that the Hawk just kept going and going. I guess compared to the venerable old Lightning that used to be in a perpetual state of maintenance, with engines giving up the ghost on a regular basis, the Hawk is in a class of its own. The Adour turbofan only came out during winter maintenance and,

more recently, if it hadn't accumulated the required number of hours, wouldn't even get its yearly visit to the engine shop at St Athan, but would go straight back into the airframe upon completion of the overhaul.

Every Hawk is different. Lined up together with parade ground precision, it is difficult to tell them apart, but they all have their own individual personalities that mark them apart. The way the engine accelerates and decelerates, the pitch and roll rates, the trim required — each pilot gets to know his own aeroplane and its idiosyncrasies by flying it day in, day out, for months at a time.

As Leader, I would generally get the old girls that had been used and abused by Synchro, and were in need of an easy season to allow the fatigue burn against flying hours ratio to return to some semblance of normality. The statistics gathered over many years proved that the Leader used the least fatigue, with the burn rate increasing the further out in the formation the aircraft normally flew. At the other end of the spectrum

Left:
Not every sky is blue — the UK summer can produce a murky day. Dark Lincolnshire provides the backdrop and streamers in this study from '4'
Opposite above:
The stem of 'Flanker' powers low and fast round the Akrotiri scrub
Opposite below left:
The Synchro Pair manoeuvre as one against a subdued cloudscape
Opposite below right:
Red sunrise

came the Synchro machines that burned enough fatigue during a winter 30-minute practice to reduce the poor old bean counters who looked after such information, to a state of apoplexy.

Even the apparently simple things can cause problems, and no part of the routine, from strapping-in to engine shut down at the end of the sortie, escapes scrutiny. Parking spaces can be very tight, and 10 or 11 aircraft finding room on an already crowded airfield can be a problem. Taxiways on most airfields are wide and generous, but the width and surface quality on some make farm tracks look like well-kept motorways. The same could be said for some runways, with a crumbling top surface, poorly maintained edges, lack of standard markings and poor over-runs all adding to the logistical headache of getting the Team in the air.

Being lined up on the runway in plenty of time is what I always aimed for. On a military field this was readily accepted by the air traffic services, but I always marvelled at the great co-operation we received from commercial airfields, who often allowed us the luxury of hogging the main strip, which sometimes delayed other paying operators.

The take-off time was worked out to the second. Exactly one minute before brakes release I called for take-off clearance which, by sticking to this protocol, allowed the rest of the guys to gird their loins, and acted as a check on my timing. Everyone checked their watches to ensure a timing cock-up wasn't about to get us into the air a minute early or late. Once cleared to take-off, I called the type of take-off, and then handed over the VHF radio to the 'nav' responsible for this particular trip. Every call I made, was always acknowledged, either by the pilot taking direct responsibility for the order, or by Red 2 if it was just an information call. For example; 'Transit take-off coming left' would always be acknowledged by the leader of the second section, normally Red 6, who as Synchro leader also led 'Gypo', the rear section on transits.

Thirty seconds before the roll, I would call 'Smoke, lights on go, power, parking brakes'. This hopefully ensured that everyone had armed their smoke master switches, turned on their nose lights as one, wound up their engines to full power to check it was available before selecting take-off thrust, and finally ensured that the parking brake was released.

It may all seem a bit Mickey Mouse, but routines like these were developed over many years to guard against our human

Opposite:
A pair of Hawks are reminiscent of playing
dolphins — looking down 'Card' from No 4
Right:
XX308 arches over in the blistering
Mediterranean midday sun

frailties, in the sure and certain knowledge that as human beings under considerable stress, we would, at some stage during the day, cock up.

The amount of thrust I selected at the front depended on the type of take-off, and sometimes the peculiarities of the airfield we were operating from. For a display take-off, I would use considerably less thrust once airborne to get everyone aboard quickly, than a transit take-off where I needed to get to 360kts quickly to keep on the timing line.

Occasionally, a short strip may mean me carrying more power than normal to ensure getting over the fence at the far end. In fact there was nearly always a fence at the far end of the runway, especially when you needed it least. I was particularly impressed by Iraklion's large concrete wall that separated the runway from the houses of the town that were built up against the far side — makes you consider your high-speed abort options!

Today though, we are heading for Plymouth Hoe from Exeter, which requires a transit across Dartmoor before displaying over the water in amongst the hills and islands that make up Plymouth's waterfront.

Shortly before the brief, the manager, who has already arrived at the show site to give the commentary and act as our safety man on the ground, phones with an update on the weather, wind, cloud, latest pressure setting, and any obstructions that he feels may not have been covered in our pre-display survey. Armed with this latest intelligence, I know that there is a slight on-shore breeze, and the cloud is broken to about half cover at about 1,500ft. We will be able to get in over the high ground of Dartmoor, and nothing that wasn't already known about is likely to cause us problems — all pretty standard stuff.

The take-off is straightforward from Exeter's reasonably long strip. Carrying about 1,100 kilos of fuel and a full

Opposite:
'Enid on the prowl', The front
section of five aircraft hug
Akrotiri's runway on the way
out to a practice

Right:
'Smithy' ready for flight — fully
kitted out the Hawk's office can
prove to be snug fit for 6ft plus
members of the Team

centreline smoke pod, my aircraft quickly reaches transit speed. The route is planned at 360kts ground speed, which means settling today at just under 375kts airspeed to counter the slight headwind. 360kts, or six miles per minute, is a comfortable compromise speed, allowing reasonable fuel economy, fairly easy navigating, and is also our average display speed. It also minimises the damage sustained by bird strikes.

Two minutes after take-off comes the first timing check, a bridge over a river passing down the left-hand side. Normally I expect to be within 10 seconds on the first fix, and then work at reducing the error over successive fixes. If there is a tailwind on the final run-in, I aim to get to the final turn-in point about 10 seconds late, allowing our greater ground speed on the final leg to ensure an accurate time on display. I guess the average over the entire season is within five seconds, which when you consider the rudimentary navigation equipment and the vagaries of the English summer weather, is a pretty good strike rate.

Having blasted across Dartmoor, said hello to the inmates of Her Majesty's prison, and found the run-in 'nav' feature, I stow my en-route map, and pick up my Ordnance Survey map, which shows a more detailed route to show centre.

Red 6 brings 'Gypo' astern and puts them into loose 'Nine

Arrow'. We have already primed our smoke systems, Red 9 has been up and reported the cloud base, and Red 8 (today's 'nav'), is liaising with the local air traffic control and reports that there are no problems and we are clear to display.

Picking out a particular road or rail junction, park, cemetery, or peculiar shaped building, I finesse the final track, whilst scanning the cloud for gaps. The timing by now is beyond my

Opposite above:
Synchro form up in stepped down
starboard echelon
Opposite below:
'Section Briefing'. Prior to the main brief, one
of the sub-sections gets its act together —
Gary Waterfall, Andy Offer, Dicky Patounis.
Right:
Gypo returns. As part of the dynamic second
half of the show, Reds 6,7,8 and 9 head down
the hill in 'Card' formation prior to splitting
into the pattern

control. If I haven't got it sorted, there is little room for redemption in the remaining few seconds. The Manager standing in his commentary position somewhere on the seafront hears our chat on his radio, and about 15 seconds out checks in and says that there is a reasonable cloud gap over crowd centre. I call the boys into close 'Nine Arrow', and then spying the gap myself quickly put them into 'Big Nine'. Staying in 'Nine Arrow' gives me unlimited options to start the show full or flat, but from 'Big Nine', there is only one way to go, and that is up.

A few seconds out I call for smoke, and now trailing the national colours as we sweep over Plymouth Hoe, I call 'pulling up'. Easing my jet into a 3.5-4 G pull, I call 'Diamond go', as soon as the 'G' is established. On this command, Synchro (Reds 6 and 7), sweep from the wings into line astern on me, and then Reds 8 and 9 on the periphery of the formation chase Reds 4 and 5 down the wing line as they close the gaps, and then slide under Reds 2 and 3 to form the signature shape of the 'Red Arrows', the 'Diamond Nine'. All of this takes but a few seconds, during which the Team changes from coloured smoke to white. However, instead of everyone smoking, only

the aircraft at the rear of the formation are left trailing diesel.

I check my speed subconsciously against pitch angle and height as we race into the vertical, and then over onto our backs, looking down at the Plymouth seafront through the hole in the cloud we have just punched through. At the top I quickly check speed and height, not that I can do a great deal about either right now, but it gives me an impression on conditions of the day and how my aircraft is performing.

Once pointing directly down at crowd centre, I call for smoke off, check the wind aloft by assessing how far we have drifted, and then twist the Team right then left to establish the 'Diamond' bend. 'Diamond' is a very versatile formation, one that you can do just about anything with. It can be looped, rolled, taken in and out of the thickest horrible cloud (well almost), and at the end of three years I felt we could have probably flown it to the Moon and back. It is also a great formation in which everyone gets chance to settle down at the beginning of the show.

Constantly trying to get a feel for the wind, I try to get the first bend at crowd centre with a fair amount of 'G' applied. Believe it or not, formation flying is often much easier with a

Above:
'Goose' – with 'Enid' flying a four, Gary Waterfall heads for the high ground, with vortices whipping the summer sky
Right:
Homesick Angels

bucket load of 'G' to contend with, rather than flying straight and level. It is far better to give the Hawk's wing something to do instead of letting it amuse itself by skipping merrily along on every piece of uneven air it can find.

Early in the training programme, when I was getting used to just how much I could safely pull and not ping the guys on the outside off into space, we were getting into some delightfully tight bends. The boys could manfully hang on as I squeezed up to between 4 and 5 'G', but occasionally the guys at the extremities had nothing left and would have to concede defeat as they felt their wings starting to enter the high 'G' stall buffet. Most of the 'roughie toughies' in the main section didn't bother with an anti-'G' suit, and on a beautifully crisp clear day, when wing and engine have lots of cold dense air to play with, some of the bends went round on very tight rails, and could last for quite a few seconds. Not being able to look at their own accelerometers, the boys would often query post flight just how much we were pulling. I would often reply that it was difficult to tell, but I did see just over 5'G' for a short time, and that they should wear their turning trousers if they were worried — none of the young blades would ever admit

defeat and besides, the 'G' suit creased the red flying suit. As a completely old duffer I think my 'G' suit was the only thing that held me together; and anyway, the pockets were handy for my spectacles and Sanatogen tablets.

After the 'Diamond' bend, I always had the option of positioning for a roll, or if the cloudbase was low, of keeping it flat with a series of flat reversals. All it took was a few seconds to think about the next couple of moves and then a short radio call. 'Going flat', or 'Going rolling' would be quickly acknowledged by Red 2, and sure that my message had gone out, all was set fair for a standard show when I could ring the

Opposite above:
'And pulling up ..... Diamond Go!' At the start of
the full show, as the 'G' settles, the team change
seamlessly into Diamond formation
from the arrival 'Big Nine'

Opposite below:
Andy Evans – focused during pre-brief

Right:
'Final Fling' — The show is over and one of the
meaner ways to arrive back at an operating base
is to loop in big battle formation. This is
particularly hard work for the guys on the
extremities, but the blood rush on the break down
the runway is worth all the heartache

changes many many times.

Today I judge the gap in the cloud is big enough to roll in, and position the boys through 'Short Diamond' into 'Big Vixen'. Reds 8 and 9 are a long way down the wing and have the hardest job staying aboard. At the centre, I pitch and roll very slowly and deliberately, trying to keep the rate constant, and a positive load on throughout. Any speeding up or slowing down of the roll rate will be multiplied many fold to the chaps on the outside. Occasionally on a smooth day, just one control input will send us all around as if flying in silky custard, but on rough days the roll rate can become a real pig. Put in the standard aileron input and the old girl hits a bump and stops, put in some more aileron to get it moving and she lurches now with increased urgency as I try and damp out the worse of the erratic lurches. I curse to myself on days such as these and marvel how the warriors far out along my extended wing-line stay in touch.

Coming out of the roll in 'Big Vixen', we pitch up changing seamlessly again to 'Short Diamond' before rolling left back down the crowd line changing to 'Eagle'. As the guys acknowledge, trailing smoke as they drift back into a shape that imitates the American Eagle fighter, I await the smoke off to be called from Red 5 who is on the outside now at the rear of the formation and can see when everyone is back in place. His call lets me manoeuvre harder to get my flightpath sorted, 'more bank and tightening' as I increase the roll and pull to keep it all close into the crowd. 'Letting it out, letting it out' as I unload the 'G' force, 'rolling out' and we are now wings level and driving downhill towards crowd centre picking up speed all the time. Judging the pull-up point with the wind of the day I call 'Smoke on go, and pulling up', and we pitch close in to the crowd showing our underbellies in 'Eagle'.

Here at Plymouth the light on shore breeze is edging the cloudbank sitting a few miles off the coast slowly towards us, but hopefully we will get most of the full show in before it cramps our style. As we establish in the near vertical, I call for a change into 'Apollo', which is immediately acknowledged by the prime movers, as the red smoke is automatically changed to white, and the whole formation shortens. 'Apollo' apes the American Moon lander, and is a beautifully tight and compressed package. In fact 'Apollo' is always a measure of a

Above:
Classic 'Diamond'
Below:
'Reds, break, break Go!!' Reds 2 and 3 are the last guys
out of the gate at the end of a flat split

particular Team's prowess, and now everyone strives for the tightest formation references.

On the downswing from the loop, I let off the backpressure to get the formation back down to 300ft and simultaneously bend it left at crowd centre. Around the back of the bend we change forward again into 'Short Diamond', before letting the wings slide back to mock the shape of civil aviation's most beautiful creation, 'Concorde'.

'Concorde' is a very long formation; requiring deft power handling to ensure the rearward retreat doesn't end up in a

fullscale rout with aircraft separated behind the main formation. On the bend as we come past crowd centre, I balance the amount of pull available. It has to be finely tuned between running the guys at the rear of the formation out of power and, on a hot day, running out of the necessary speed and energy required to be able to loop once we have rolled out.

I try and maintain 360kts for the loops, but know that I can use 340 as an absolute cut-off. Being slow into the pull means being low and slow over the top, which in extremis, is the worst possible place to be.

Today the air pressure is up, and the temperature typically moderate, so performance isn't a big player and we roll out of 'Concorde' heading out to sea before pulling up once again into a loop, changing into 'Feathered Arrow'. Now 'Feathered Arrow' is a real mouthful, so it is known in the trade as 'Fred'. The front four aircraft move forward to join me, as Reds 8 and 9 move forward onto Red 7's wing, who is the rearmost man in the central stem. All of this must be done symmetrically, with both sides of the formation moving as one.

At the end of the 'Fred' loop, I bend the formation right, and once settled with the right bank and 'G' load applied, I call the move into 'Tango' for the final big roll of the first half of the

Above:
"Thoroughbreds together". An immaculately preserved P-51 of the Intrepid Aviation Company, flown by Norman Lees, leads Synchro into the blue

Below:
All nine aircraft safely airborne, Reds 4 and 5 slot on to the outside of the front vic, whilst Gypo try to escape the dirty air a few hundred metres astern

Above:
Chasing their shadows, the Synchro '98 ('Stobes' and 'Cubes') keep it low

competing against Red 6 to find the gaps in the cloud big enough to get my formation through. Frequently, we would clip the edges of summer cumulus to get the sun glinting off the paintwork for a few fleeting seconds as we rocketed up into the clear bit of summer that those on the ground were missing, before gravity dragged us back through the same ragged hole to rejoin the mere mortals living below the perpetual summer overcast.

We finish the show on a blistering formation break, showering multi-coloured smoke and ear splitting jet noise, before rejoining into two sections for the run home.

Leaving Plymouth we head back over the moors and then East towards Exeter. Red 8 is already liaising with Exeter airport to allow us to rejoin, and

show. This manoeuvre is incredibly difficult for Reds 2 to 5, or so they tell me, with the boys flying line abreast throughout the roll. My job as ever is to fly a slow, evenly loaded roll, without varying the roll rate, get the positioning right, fly and speak on the radio at the same time, whilst avoiding the ground.

Once we have got ourselves in the front section sorted into 'Big Five', 'Gypo' (Reds 6,7,8 and 9 who have split away from us and rolled the opposite way), position behind us in readiness for the second half of the show. I won't get to see Synchro on my wing again until the run home, and only occasionally meet up with Reds 8 and 9 as they spend their time flitting between sections.

I enjoy all parts of the show, but the second half is far more dynamic, and my interest level increases. I now watch and listen to Synchro blathering on as they race at one another, and try to position 'Enid' in between, thus minimising any gaps.

In fairness, the boys in 'Gypo', and particularly the Synchro pair, put on an awesome show, not only making the impossible look easy, but also maintaining this standard show after show.

Again we have the option of mixing full, rolling and flat routines, and I always enjoyed the added bit of spice of

eventually they negotiate with London control, who administer the airway above, to allow us to loop if we wish. Never one to turn down the chance to grab one final aerobatic manoeuvre, we gather together again as one big red machine as we overfly the field before pulling up into a glorious loop, trailing what smoke we have left. Then down and down, hard and fast, down the runway before peeling away individually into the downwind landing pattern.

Once stopped on the runway and the last guy down calls that he is safely under control, we collectively pull in our landing flaps, switch off our lights, and taxi back in formation, before being marshalled with parade ground precision onto our parking slots.

The whole sortie probably lasted but 45 minutes. Dozens of letters, hours of planning, intricate map work, innumerable telephone calls, and now it is just another show completed. We watch the video of our performance as soon as we can after the show, picking out the areas for improvement. There is always something to work on, and everyone has a voice in the debrief, and nobody is above constructive criticism, especially the Leader.

Opposite:
Easing it up – The Boss – John Rands, leads the 'Twizzle' over Lincolnshire
Right:
Tearing moisture out the air the Reds pull a 3 'G' manoeuvre

Painting the Heavens Red

At the end of September '96 it was all over. After a few days away in the Mediterranean and a long transit back through Europe, I eased my aircraft onto the Boss' parking spot at Cranwell and pulled the throttle back through the cut off to silence the Adour for the last time. I had survived nearly 17 years of continuous military flying and from now on I would be flying a desk to see out my final few months of service. I was elated, relieved, dreading retirement and probably more tired than I could imagine. It had been a magnificent roller-coaster of a ride that had lived up to all of the RAF recruiting slogans that had enticed me 20 years before. Yes I had seen the World, yes I had flown the latest and hottest ships, and yes I have seen and done many things that some can only dream about.

Looking back through my logbooks I flew well over 2,000 'Red Arrows' sorties, over 2,000 hours flying in the Hawk, and over 600 public displays in 35 countries across four continents.

If I have talked lovingly about inanimate pieces of machinery, then it is because in the hands of the right people these machines come to life. Witnessing the incredible flying skill, dedication, and full-hearted love for life of the many I have been privileged to fly alongside, has left an indelible mark on me.

I will remember many of the places that I have visited, and I will remember with great satisfaction the aeroplanes that I have flown, but most of all, when everything is said and done, I will remember the people.

For those who guided me in my formative years and gave me the confidence to believe that all things are possible, I give thanks. For those who served with me over the years, through the good times (mostly) and the bad times (occasionally), I value above all else the friendship that has been so freely given. For the guys who worked for me during my last tour with the Reds, I can never fully repay the trust and belief that you showed in me. I could try from now to the end of time, but some debts can never be repaid. Thank You. ✈

Left:
Framing Red 1 in the MDC
Above:
Synchro about to cross and pull up for the 'Opposition Loop'
Opposite:
Best of British: Concorde and the Reds framed by lush green fields during the 50th Anniversary of Heathrow flypast 2 June 1996

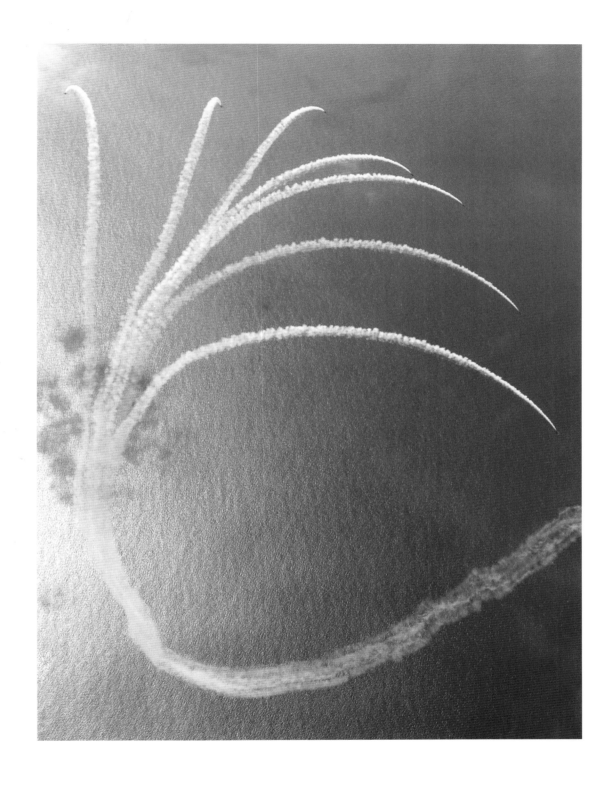

REDS

Formations

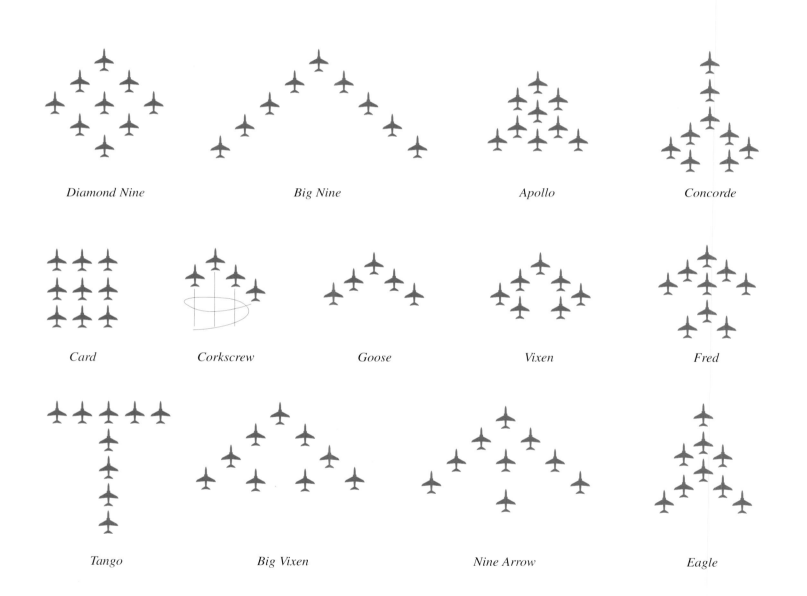

Diamond Nine   *Big Nine*   *Apollo*   *Concorde*

Card   *Corkscrew*   *Goose*   *Vixen*   *Fred*

Tango   *Big Vixen*   *Nine Arrow*   *Eagle*